Building Brand
with
Direct Response
Television

Building Brand with Direct Response Television

Freeing this Powerful Modern Medium
from the Shackles of Yell & Sell
and the Misperceptions
of Traditional Advertising

by *Doug Garnett*

Founder & CEO, Atomic Direct
Portland, OR

ATOMIC
DIRECT

Many of the articles in this publication were originally published in *Response Magazine* 2004-2011.

Response Magazine: The Only Independent Source for Direct Response Marketers. www.ResponseMag.com

ISBN-13: 978-0-61546-797-9
ISBN-10: 0-61546-797-0

Printed in the United States of America

10 9 8 7 6 5 4 3 2 1

Cover art used with permission by Timothy C. Ely

Design by Ann Marra

Illustrations by Don Lewis

Published by
Atomic Direct, LTD
1219 SE Lafayette Street • Portland, OR 97202
503.296.6131
www.atomicdirect.com

Dedicated to Judith

Table of Contents

Storyboards, Illustrations, and Case Studies

Introduction

*How Did a Nice Guy Like You End Up
As an Infomercial Expert?*

At 8:00 pm EST on October 28, 2008, infomercials grew up. That's when the Obama presidential campaign's prime time infomercial sealed his election with simultaneous half hour airings across five networks that amassed an estimated thirty-three million viewers. The infomercial was cleverly conceived and well produced. And while other advertisers should use infomercials to deliver more "break through" messages, the campaign wisely used communications that chose not to risk Mr. Obama's lead with only five days until the election.

What may be lost on the more casual observer is how much this infomercial broke away from the formulas that even brand DRTV providers typically follow. Obviously, there was no tacky call-to-action and he never offered free merchandise for immediate action. Instead, his team treated the half hour for what it is – a tremendous opportunity to deliver messages that wouldn't otherwise be possible.

It worked. From what I read, the infomercial influenced Republicans and independents alike. It strengthened the resolve of his Democratic supporters. And considering pre- and post-infomercial poll results, it appears that the Obama infomercial played a key role consolidating Mr. Obama's lead to put him over the top to become the 44th President of the United States.

I began my career as a mathematician on space and military projects. But my love of communication led me out of the back room with a stint as a supercomputer salesman and finally into television advertising. It was an accidental path. But it led me into a fascinating business with tremendous opportunity to drive deeper and find new ways to leverage infomercials and their short form counterparts to help clients build successful companies.

Despite DRTV's tremendous opportunity, it remains disappointing that TV screens are too often filled with the crass silliness of traditional yell & sell. And it's even more disappointing that the traditional world of brands and advertising remains stuck in out-of-date perceptions of infomercials. So I've pulled together this book to take another step forward in articulating the brand power of this unique medium.

My work in DRTV started in 1993 when I joined The Tyee Group where I became their vice president of strategy. Tyee was the leading brand DRTV producer at the time so I worked with an amazing array of outstanding brands. But most importantly, I learned important lessons about the things that don't work in DRTV. Our work tried so hard to look like "regular advertising" that it was rarely persuasive enough to drive action.

When I founded my own agency in 1998, my goal was to deliver dramatically more DRTV impact to brand advertisers. We've done that – leading the way with smart, savvy, and informative DRTV that sells while building brand. And we've done this with an unusual array of products the traditional business would have rejected – establishing many DRTV "firsts".

As you start this book, let me ask that you open your mind to one key possibility. Businesses seek "game changing" opportunity. While new media claims to offer this change, it lacks the muscle needed by mass marketers. Traditional advertising claims to change the game with creativity. But that leads to the extremes of elite art – extremes which fail to communicate with the real people who purchase products.

Direct Response Television is one of very few communication opportunities that can truly change the game. DRTV makes major change happen quickly. DRTV can quickly reposition your brand. DRTV can rebuild profit margins. DRTV opens doors at retail. DRTV drives new product introductions faster and broader than any other medium. And, even better, only DRTV can do this while delivering extraordinary measurements of campaign effectiveness. ▼

A Note about Organization

This book brings together my articles, blog posts, and DRTV work – particularly from the past decade. This means that I have chosen NOT to follow the all-too-common format of the modern business book. (My experience of modern business books finds they start with a couple valuable chapters then spend their remaining pages re-telling you what they've already told you.)

With this difference, I hope this book offers new surprises and insights throughout. And, I hope that while this book can be read from front to back it can also be used by readers to explore topics when those topics will give you the most value.

*"The more informative your advertising,
the more persuasive it will be."*

DAVID OGILVY

The Hidden Power of Direct Response Television

Despite a history of driving change at lower cost than traditional TV, Direct Response Television (DRTV) remains misunderstood and underutilized. In part, the term "infomercial" implies an all-too-often seen cheesy TV ad that uses exaggerated promises to sell low quality product.

But after twenty years, I have come to use the term "infomercial" proudly. This broad medium of DRTV can drive positive change for your company and your brand faster, and with better financial results, than almost any other advertising.

The following section starts with the fundamental questions about today's television – responding to those who would claim that TV is dead. With this foundation in place, we discuss the two types of DRTV (short form and long form) and round out the section looking at DRTV's ability to build brands.

Underlying this discussion is my single-minded focus on executing powerful DRTV in ways that build your brand and drives profit – without ever raising that gimmicky feeling you might get from an ad for a ShamWow, Shake Weight, or Snuggie.

Research Shows TV is as Powerful as It's Ever Been

Before exploring DRTV, we need to consider the health of the TV business. Current hype from the kings of digital media might lead some to believe that TV is going away. In fact, it isn't. And TV is stronger today than it's ever been.

The first time we were told to expect the death of television advertising was from fears that remote controls and the VCR would put advertisers out of business (they didn't). When DVRs appeared over ten years ago, we were once again told that TV advertising would die (it didn't). Now the "TV killer" idea is trotted out for every new media option – from "buzz" marketing and YouTube to social networking and mobile advertising.

Fortunately, in order to sort media fact from fiction, the Journal of Advertising Research (JAR) dedicated its June 2009 edition to new and old media options. It includes articles dedicated to specific media types as well as compendium articles looking at how to balance an integrated media mix. What they found is surprising.

Television Advertising's Impact Is Increasing

This is a jaw-dropping conclusion. And the studies are very clear: TV advertising is increasing in impact.

For example, one article reports findings that one index of TV effectiveness has increased 30% from 2005 to 2008 (The Dratfield Analysis). This same article reports a 50% increase in the television "Persuasion Points" between 1997 and 2006 according to the ARS database.[*]

---

[*] Joel Rubinson. "Empirical Evidence of TV Advertising Effectiveness," Journal of Advertising Research, Vol. 49. No. 2. www.journalofadvertisingresearch.com, June 2009

Another team of authors concludes, "TV will remain the preeminent fast and vast advertising medium."[*]

TV Viewership Has Not Declined

We were told to expect TV's decline because viewership would decline. In fact, it's not declining. The latest studies find that TV consumption is as high as ever. During primetime on any given evening you will still find two thirds of American households watching TV.

Attention While Viewing TV Has Not Decreased

We've also been told that TV advertising will lose impact because viewers are "multi-tasking" – watching TV while browsing the Internet or playing their Nintendo DS.

In fact, there is no drop in effectiveness of TV advertising. My own sense is that we've always multi-tasked while watching. Thirty years ago, my college roommate and I played darts during commercial breaks while watching *M*A*S*H* every night. Is anything really different today? We have new options for distraction, but they're just replacing the old distractions – not the TV viewing.

TV Effectiveness Hasn't Decreased Due to DVRs

DVRs were supposed to put the nail in the coffin of TV advertising. The JAR studies look at this question and find no drop in effectiveness due to DVRs.

Why? One study notes that without DVRs, we saw three types of behavior during commercial breaks: one-third of viewers remain active viewers, one-third partially view commercials, and one-third completely avoids commercials.

It appears this behavior remains the same with DVRs and that their impact is to allow people who would have ignored the advertising anyway to fast forward past it.

Television Makes Other Media Work Better

The JAR studies also show that when a TV campaign is on-air, other media have higher impact as well. The direct response television (DRTV) business should take note. While television might be our core communication, it has even more impact when used with other media. Building a solid foundation of communication with TV makes for better success, for example, in word of mouth advertising campaigns (this is just one cross-media finding in the JAR articles).

---

[*] Byron Sharp, Virginia Beal, Martin Collins. "Television: Back to the Future," Journal of Advertising Research, Vol. 49, No. 2. www.journalofadvertisingresearch.com, June 2009

Why Do We Hear So Much About New Media?

New media dominates discussion right now because it benefits three power centers. First, it's good for advertising agencies. In broad terms, it shifts client spending from media expense to agency manpower – the best source of agency profit.

New media hype is also good for new media companies. These companies stand to make billions from successful IPOs or acquisitions. Finally, new media is good for journalists. It gives the 24-hour cable news cycle and traditional advertising reporters a topic that drives viewership and readership – their key to profits.

Unfortunately none of these groups are the advertisers themselves. Truth is, new media has had more impact on agency profits than in generating profits for clients.

Back to the Future with DRTV

Far from the death of television, these studies show that television's evolution gives it amazing vitality and life. DRTV is one of those sources of TV's vitality – an evolution that brings new power to advertisers with campaigns that can be mounted for pennies on the TV dollar.

Only one question remains for advertisers: When will you make DRTV the core of your advertising? ▼

Other Findings

The Biggest Impact of Online Advertising Is at the Store

One of these studies found that the biggest profit potential for online advertising is sales at offline sources like retail. It works like this: Online, you have a limited universe you are able to reach. But offline you have dramatically more opportunity for people to purchase based on your online advertising. So, in fact, the potential for profit from online advertising comes at the retail store. Interesting.

Traditional TV Brand Rules Still Need to Be Followed

Many times I've heard creative teams justify bad creative choices by saying that the consumer is so savvy today that we don't need to follow old brand principals. In just one example, these studies confirmed again that on average fully 60% of viewers can not recall the brand names of the advertising they watched. The fix is simple. The research further found that visual repetition of the brand name was required to increase recall of the brand.

Product Innovation Substantially Increases Advertising Impact

Those of us in DRTV shouldn't be surprised by this one. The traditional advertising business would do well to pay more attention to this. The mistake many traditional brand advertising campaigns make is trying to leverage *creative innovation* when much bigger impact would come from clearly communicating *product innovation*.

Long Form:
What Can Infomercials Do
for Your Brand?

In the US, long form DRTV commercials are typically 28:30 in length. They ask the viewer to take action by calling an 800-number, visiting a website, and/or responding via mobile phone. Some are also tagged for retail stores.

Consumer giants increasingly use short form DRTV to raise awareness of their products. Surprisingly, they haven't embraced long form – or half hour – programs as readily.

So I asked long-time clients and experienced half hour users Dave Merten and Kevin Blodgett for their thoughts. After all, today's half hour infomercials provide a unique tool for the brand marketer – the opportunity to make innovative, complex, and highly-profitable products sell while building brand.

Their answer? Lacking half hour experience, few corporations understand where to start, what can be achieved, or how to create successful half hours.

Half Hours Fill Retail Gaps

Today, you'll find Dave developing lawn and garden products that his business sells through retail channels. His infomercial experience started as director of marketing at Bissell and expanded as VP of Merchandising at Newell/Rubbermaid's Mirro division. "Companies need to realize that infomercials are the magic ingredient for unique, higher-end products with high retail value," Dave observed. "Remember there's no longer someone in the stores doing demos, so you can't just put a ground-breaking product on a retail shelf and expect it to sell."

Kevin's experience with the half hour format started when he joined Professional Tool Manufacturing (ProTool), manufacturers of Drill Doctor the drill bit sharpener. "I'd been VP of Marketing for Famous Footwear so had an extensive understanding of traditional advertising. But when I started with ProTool, I knew nothing about DRTV and disliked infomercials." Kevin has now spent years implementing a strategy that includes long form DRTV.

"It has been a real learning experience for me because long form DRTV is very different from traditional advertising," continued Kevin. "My perceptions have turned 180 degrees – our half hour infomercials are critical to our retail success. Drill Doctor is not an intuitive product. It takes time to show customers how it works. Long form DRTV gives us that time."

Kevin's experience is not unusual. In the late 1990s, Philips Consumer Electronics spent $11M on traditional :30 spots introducing WebTV, but the inventory sat on shelves. Then they created a half hour infomercial. After only $2M to $3M in spending, they had to pull the infomercial because the product sold out at retail.

Clearly, marketers need to change any out-of-date perceptions about infomercials and infomercial quality. Said Kevin, "Until we ask for the order, our infomercial is simply great programming about sharpening drill bits and doing your work." Dave concurred. "Research shows that the branded infomercials we've developed aren't even considered infomercials by consumers. They're simply long forms of advertising."

Half Hours Make Complicated Products Succeed

Further, Dave noted that many products that would flourish with infomercials are rejected because typical product evaluations filter them out. "It is sad to me when companies recognize a need for complex or difficult communication on a viable product, and reject the product. As a consultant, I see this all the time – it's unnecessary."

....

Work Sharp Infomercial

This infomercial had to convince consumers of the benefits of this radically different benchtop grinder. And the core difference was shifting the wheel from vertical to flat – opening up an amazing array of value. This graphic was used throughout the paid program to establish the key difference: the flat wheel.

Put a new spin on grinding and sharpening

Standard market research tests for new product viability are part of the problem. Kevin noted "most companies would have abandoned Drill Doctor based on early 'top two box' scores." ProTool persevered, and they've sold over two million sharpeners – a $100 product that sharpens a 25-cent drill bit.

Dave noted that advertising agencies share the blame for companies avoiding infomercials. "Most company's ad agencies don't understand infomercials any better than their clients do, so if there's a product that needs more time to deliver a complex message, they recommend rejecting the product," he said. Or worse, they proceed with the product and waste scarce advertising dollars creating :30 spots for a product that needs a half hour infomercial to succeed. It pays to have an experienced DRTV agency on your side – as Dave observed, "It's not as easy as it may look to get it right."

Half Hours Build Margins

Consider this regular complaint: "The buyer says Home Depot won't stock my product at a price any higher than X."

The infomercial is your opportunity to regain margin.

Look at the experience of Dave's Wearever Allegro team. They sold square cookware on TV for $400 when traditional products sold at retail for closer to $100. With the price point benchmarked, they then rolled the product into retail and were able to maintain high margins. Kevin has duplicated this success with Drill Doctor.

Few companies can afford to put a live demonstrator in 3,000 stores at once today. With a half hour show, the value is built in the retail consumer's mind before they walk in the store.

Half Hours Deliver Solid Numbers

"What I like about DRTV is that one can spend just a bit of money and get data immediately," continued Dave. "It doesn't cost much to try it and see what happens, sometimes even if you're still in prototype."

Take Drill Doctor. They released their first half hour in November 2001. With relatively low investment over the next six months, this show so impacted the market that by June of 2002, over a third of retail purchasers had first learned about Drill Doctor on the infomercial.

Kevin observed, "We now have a three-pronged approach that includes long form DRTV. Consumers see the infomercial, hear about Drill Doctor on the radio, see a print ad, an article or maybe an in-store ad, think 'oh, I've seen that,' and buy it. It's exciting to watch the process work."

A half hour did great things for Netpliance's iOpener (an Internet appliance), who spent widely on Circuit City distribution, a Super Bowl spot, and weekly Parade Magazine ads, plus a small amount on an infomercial. Even after it was off-air for four months (during which time the other media continued), the infomercial remained the third largest sales channel, and the cost per unit was one tenth what it cost to sell through the other channels.

Kevin is optimistic for infomercials. "I encourage newbies to be open to this approach, recognize and set aside any pre-conceived notions, and evaluate what long form DRTV can do for your business. We're sure glad we did." ▼

Short Form:
TV Advertising with
an Outstanding ROI

*Short form DRTV spots are 30, 60, or 120 seconds in length
and ask the viewer to call an 800-number, visit a website,
and/or respond via mobile phone.*

Brand advertisers often begin their DRTV adventure with short form because it looks, feels, and smells very much like traditional television advertising. And, compared with long form, short form would seem to involve less risk for their brand.

The truth is that short form is a good place for brands to start. But be careful. Short form's comfort and familiarity also leads brands astray. In fact, some brands do no more than add an 800-number to a traditional TV spot then call it DRTV. Other brands hire DRTV agencies who create little more than traditional TV spots broadcast with traditional media schedules. In either case, these approaches miss out on DRTV's potential.

Brand advertisers need, instead, to embrace short form for its unique power before they can tap deeply into DRTV's power to drive sales and build brand.

Creative Power: The Product Is the Star

Short form's key difference comes from measuring how well your advertising moves consumers to action. You can't measure traditional TV advertising's ability to drive action – so this is a unique opportunity made possible by DRTV.

What we learn from this measurement is that *product value motivates far more action than brand promise.* This approach is much different from the brand advertising taught in universities and portfolio schools these days. So, brand creative teams rarely know how to drive action.

Fortunately, when you make the product your star, you also make your brand the star. Consumers retain brand communication better when a product personifies

CSAA "Drycleaner" DRTV :60

(Open on a man chasing his out-of-control car down the street)

VO: The wrong time to think about car insurance is when you need it most. Meet Jill. Jill has AAA auto insurance. Jill knows that her AAA Insurance is just as dependable as the Emergency Roadside Service she gets from AAA.

VO: So if you've been wondering about your insurance, call us for a quote today and find out how additional coverage options make auto insurance from AAA more affordable than ever.

VO: And with over ninety years of insurance experience, AAA has seen it all.

SFX: (sound of crash, exclamation)

VO: So, if Jill ever does have a claim, she knows her AAA insurance team is dedicated to getting her vehicle repaired and back on the road…just like it never happened.

VO: Call right now or visit your local AAA office for a no-obligation auto insurance quote and you'll get this complimentary accident claim kit, just for getting a quote!

VO: This kit includes a disposable camera, information check-list, a flashlight, and more…because AAA wants you to be prepared – for whatever the road brings you. Call AAA insurance now...And on you go.

This spot was created with footage from a traditional 30-second brand spot. And it won Best in Show – Television at the IMCA awards beating out Allstate's advertisements with actor Dennis Haysbert. Why? We think it's because the ad was motivating.

the brand values because consumers buy products that have brands – they don't buy brands.

Media Power: The Hidden Secret

Short form's creative power is complemented by an equivalent media power.

Bought correctly, short form DRTV is placed within programming like traditional TV, but falls into a special rate class for remnant time. As a result, it is purchased at a dramatic discount because you give stations flexibility in placing the spots. (A typical weekly order to a station might ask for ten airings between noon and 4:00 pm spread across Monday through Friday.)

How much is the discount? Big. Remnant time is inexpensive – perhaps discounted 50% to 75% when compared to costs for traditional TV. But that's just the start.

In buying DRTV time, traditional planning and buying approaches play only a minor role. The best DRTV buyers put their efforts into finding the media time that delivers the most phone or web orders (or calls) per dollar. As a result, DRTV gains another two to four times impact – impact you'll never find with traditional planning.

And most importantly, the stations that drive the highest response by web or phone also drive the best response through other sales channels like retail.

Does Short Form Meet Your Strategic Needs?

Just like long form, short form offers tremendous opportunities for brands – but a different set of opportunities.

Long form offers unique power to bring complex products to market while supporting high margins. Short form, by contrast, gives you a highly flexible approach for building brand power and lets you do this with a wider array of products.

Consider how important direct sales are for you. If you're looking for immediate direct sales, your product's price will determine format. The general rule is that short form products need to be impulse priced – at or below $25. By contrast, long form directly sells products priced as high as $1,000 and higher.

And remember, if you need long form, short form won't work. Consider our campaigns for the Drill Doctor and the Kreg Jig. Both use long form because the communication that moves people to action takes too much time to be executed with short form.

Also, be careful of your assumptions. It's a mistake to opt for short form by assuming there's no way to create compelling long form shows for your products. Don't be sure. In our Drill Doctor infomercial we deliver thirty minutes of compelling communication about drill bits and the show was so effective it ran for eight years.

Short Form Delivers

When you take advantage of short form DRTV's full power, amazing things happen. But most importantly, you'll discover a new type of TV ad that drives immediate and measurable action while also building long-term brand value. That means that companies who conquer this medium can leverage short form DRTV to achieve surprising power for their brand. ▼

The Rich World of Short Form

Short form DRTV opens a world of marketing opportunity. Here's a brief list of some principal ways companies use short form to build their business.

• Drive sales at retail (or any channel) while also selling directly.

• Open a new sales channel directly to consumers.

• Generate leads that turn into sales via direct mail and phone, through your sales force, through B2B distributors, or through retail.

• Drive website or mobile marketing traffic.

• Increase sales through your online store.

Building Brands
One Product at a Time

We were reviewing results from one of our DRTV campaigns at a recent client meeting. It was an absolutely exceptional campaign – blew the doors off at retail, direct sales were superb, and Internet buzz was excellent.

Hanging in the air of the room, though, is a kind of funny question: How can this be good branding? After all, it sold so well.

Use Products to Build Brand

This question shouldn't surprise any of us. Traditional agencies have spent decades convincing clients not to expect immediate results from their brand advertising. But what we need to realize is that so-called "brand advertising" is just one method for building brand.

There are many ways to build brand – including with DRTV. And when done correctly, DRTV offers a unique opportunity to make big brand change happen quickly. Because DRTV's brand power comes from a focus on product.

Brand While You Sell and Sell While You Brand

The power of product advertising to build brand can be quickly seen from a small set of truths:

Products Showcase Brand Value. Product is the strongest way to personify brand values. So when you are building a new brand or need to cause a dramatic shift in perception of your brand, you'll create the largest change – fastest – when you bring products to the forefront to lead that charge.

Products Are Humanly Powerful. People are people. And they don't buy visions – they buy products. Too much brand advertising offers a brand vision that never sinks into viewer consciousness because it's delivered without evidence. But when you show how the product showcases the vision, then it's easier to remember the vision and to believe the product will deliver it.

Product Value Increases the Price Consumers Will Pay Far More Than Brand. Perceived brand value generally adds between 5% and 25% to the price of the product (sometimes as high as 50%). By contrast, clearly articulated product value easily adds 100%, 200%, or more to this price. (And the highest perceived value comes when product value and brand are combined.)

Emotions Close to a Product Are Most Powerful. Account planning has led traditional advertising into a wilderness of obscure emotion. But in truth, it's the emotions close to the product that drive purchase and drive brand power.

Products Build Trust In Brand Promises. Brands build trust through a cycle of promise and delivery. Consumers who buy directly see the promise delivered most quickly. Even better, DRTV creative is so action oriented it drives consumers to retail much more quickly than when driven by other advertising. In either case, this shortened trust cycle is powerful for your brand.

A Product's Story Is Naturally Memorable. Brand ads work hard (often too hard) to make memorable statements. But messages centered on products are easier for consumers to remember – making them the ones that drive consumer action.

DRTV Media Costs Are Also a Branding Advantage

DRTV's brand power doesn't all happen in the creative. Because no matter how powerful your creative, it isn't building brand when it's off-air.

When you buy DRTV, you are buying remnant media at dramatically reduced price. Then, profits from on-air sales can subsidize some (or all) of your media costs.

....

Kobalt Tools' Multi-Drive Wrench campaign took advantage of all six degrees of DRTV. This, combined with a fully integrated campaign including web, circulars and customer service agents produced superb results. ➤

Kobalt Tools
Multi-Drive Wrench
1:20

HOST: Sometimes just finding the right tool is half the job. But at Kobalt we realized it could be much easier… and developed

…this. The Kobalt Multi-Drive Wrench.

The heads of the Multi-Drive rotate. Giving you eight sockets on one wrench…

each designed to fit both standard and metric sizes.

Kobalt's Multi-Drive uses a socket style popular among aircraft and racecar mechanics. Each socket works on hex and square bolts, as well as three types of high precision bolts…even if they're rounded or damaged.

So one Multi-Drive is like having fifty six sockets in your tool bag.

Buy your Kobalt Multi-Drive today for just $24.97. The one wrench that handles standard and metric sizes, as well as six types of bolt heads.

Your Multi-Drive comes with an additional driver head that works on all driver bits and standard sockets…Kobalt Multi-Drive is the perfect wrench around the home or on the go.

The result is that DRTV makes each media dollar go as much as two to eight times farther. So if you were going to spend $4M on traditional media, with DRTV you can often expand that spending to $8M in media buys which deliver $16M worth of traditional media value. That's a lot of impact.

Creating DRTV That Builds Brand

As you create brand DRTV, you'll need to balance two fundamental realities in order to get the brand value you want. First, avoid the trappings of yell & sell. This may seem obvious. But many so-called "brand DRTV agencies" use hard-sell techniques in their brand DRTV work – techniques that not only hurt your brand but drive away retail business.

At the same time, other agencies create pretty pictures that don't sell. Don't ever be afraid to sell your product. Consumers expect you to sell. And they want you to do so with honest, clear, and meaningful communication that avoids the hype and exaggeration of yell & sell.

Proven Brand Power

What do brands like Kobalt Tools, Sears/Craftsman, Tempur-Pedic, Bose, The Home Depot, Angie's List, eHarmony, ProForm Fitness, Bowflex, GoToMeeting, Hamilton Beach, GEICO, and Nationwide all have in common? Each of these has used DRTV to help build their brand.

Even in the largest corporations, DRTV should sit at the brand table as an equal partner. And if you can afford both brand TV and DRTV, your brand advertising should make the broad brand promises while DRTV should show how the products deliver on the promise.

But branding with DRTV isn't just for the big players. Our eight-year campaign for the Drill Doctor drill bit sharpener built a surprisingly strong national brand for a tiny company with a niche product. And even the smallest entrepreneur should look at their DRTV work to ensure that it lays a brand foundation that returns future profit.

So go for it. Create your future with brand building, product focused DRTV. And never again question whether you can brand while you sell. ▼

Cable TV Becomes Trackable With DRTV

Co-written with Dan Zifkin, President of Zephyr Media
and longtime friend of Atomic Direct

Traditional or mainstream TV is a powerful medium. An estimated 100 million households in the US watch the four major networks. But traditional TV tends to deliver measurable advertising results only for true mass-market products – in part because you need about $15M to begin even the smallest mainstream TV campaign.

Cable TV, on the other hand, is a powerfully viable alternative, delivering much higher ROIs on much lower budgets in a national campaign. With cable TV, significant impact can be seen from as little as $500K in media spending. Why?

- Specialized audiences have emerged from "topical networks" like Speed Channel, E!, and more. This opens a golden opportunity for niche products to reach the viewers who want to know about – and more importantly buy – them.

- The large number of cable networks (100 and growing) means you can get superb media deals with emerging networks – if you negotiate the right bargain.

New Planning Approaches

But, to get high impact with small budgets on cable TV, you need to change the way you plan and execute TV campaigns – to include response measured advertising. Because only measuring consumer response to your advertisement will ensure that you're reaching these specialized audiences in a cost effective way and getting the best deals on cable TV media.

In other words, you need to combine traditional planning methods with DRTV. In fact, relying on response measurements can increase impact (ROI) per media dollar by four to ten times – using that $500K budget to deliver equivalent impact of $5M spent through traditional media planning.

Three Myths About Cable and TV

Three key myths persist in media planning that affect your ability to maximize cable TV ROI.

It's important to understand these myths, and the truth about them, if you're to take advantage of cable's potential.

Myth: Brands can only be built around traditional advertising.

Truth: DRTV is a very cost-effective way to create and build a brand – whether you decide to just generate leads or to generate sales as well. Experience shows that a targeted DRTV campaign is highly effective at building brand recognition. Plus, while you are generating visibility, you can also generate sales that impact your bottom line with a higher ROI. In fact, cable TV provides the most cost-effective brand medium in television today.

Myth: You can use Nielsen data with cable just like you can on major networks.

Truth: A tremendous amount of cable TV falls into the "too-small-to-be-measured" category. Reliable Nielsen data is only available for the large cable networks and often only for primetime programming. However, many of the best deals on cable are on smaller, emerging networks with audiences too small to generate significant Nielsen ratings. Unfortunately, many traditional agencies make the mistake of taking whatever numbers they can find about a given network and providing them to clients without knowing whether they're valid. Measuring response ensures that you know what impact you're getting from your media.

Myth: A "hot" cable show has a massive audience.

Truth: Cable audiences are smaller than you might think. Even the hottest shows have relatively small audiences. For example, the popular "American Chopper" typically has an audience of less than 800,000 (compare this with thirteen million viewers for "Survivor"). This is good news for niche advertisers. Smaller channels comprise viewers who are actively interested in the subject matter, and therefore more likely to purchase related goods and services. Plus smaller channels are hungry for ad dollars, so they are more willing to negotiate very favorable terms. In fact, it is the small – and specialized – nature of the audience that makes them an attractive DRTV outlet.

Our Experience with DuPont Teflon

DuPont's Teflon coating can be seen as a "Kleenex" product that buyers take for granted. So DuPont needed to reignite consumer interest and make their products distinct from other non-stick surfaces.

In 2005 we delivered a DRTV campaign highlighting cookware coated with their newest product, Teflon with Radiance Technology. Traditional media planning demographics indicated that Home & Garden (HGTV) and Food Network should be primary in our media plan. However, after we put it on air, we watched the volume of phone calls and saw that HGTV and Food shows were four to eight times less effective at moving consumers to action. This is in part because of the premium charged by the national channels and in part because traditional demographics can't show whether the consumers who watch are purchase-ready. It turns out that many more cookware *buyers* watch Soap Net and Lifetime Movie!

The key to success was a coupon-driven campaign for which we combined TV, Internet, and retail, because the coupon allowed us to measure the media's effectiveness. The resulting data identified which cable channel generated which level of response, resulting in hard numbers to verify cost-effectiveness. And, since DRTV can be purchased on short notice, we were able to change the campaign on the fly to eliminate the media that didn't produce cost-effective results.

As a result of this campaign, higher-margin cookware sets – instead of individual pots – became the hot sellers, because the DRTV spot established the uniqueness of Teflon's new surface and the coupon drove purchases of sets. Even better, our follow-on research showed that more people believed the promise made about Teflon than typically believe promises made in traditional brand advertising. ▼

Integrating DRTV with Direct Mail

Television and direct mail have often lived in an uneasy relationship. This is unfortunate, because these two mediums offer tremendous benefits when used in tandem.

TV offers direct mail practitioners two critical benefits. First, its communication power is unequalled. So when you need to break through in your communication, television is often the best option. Television is also unique in "reaching out" to consumers by introducing them to products they'd never considered before.

TV Doesn't Have To Be On-Air To Have Impact

Let me be clear that all forms of television are helpful for direct mail – on-air, in the mail, and online. Even niche categories can benefit from the unique TV opportunity.

For example, the mailed DVD can have more impact than its online counterpart. Why? In part, online transmission typically loses more than half of TV's communication power. Online transmission fails too often. But perhaps even more importantly, a DVD is a physical item that carries your message merely by its existence.

In a B2B campaign, Graham Medical used TV to help introduce the MegaMover Transport Chair, a compact, disposable patient transporter for paramedics. Potential purchasers were sent a DVD, a trial offer, and directed to distributors. The DVD not only got their attention, but the DVD was passed to the approval chain – usually a safety committee. Because these committees had physical DVDs, they saw more persuasive TV and viewed it in a more persuasive environment – as a team.

Video and Direct Mail— The Dynamic Duo

Emails and links to YouTube are often ignored. If you send a DVD to your prospective consumer it will be passed along inside a business. This means your demonstration is seen by the entire group of decision makers.

My agency produced a direct mailer and sales DVD for the MegaMover® Transport Chair by Graham Medical™ (division of Little Rapids Corp.). The Transport Chair is a strong, disposable alternative for EMTs, fire departments and nursing home staff to use when carrying patients down stairs and through narrow hallways – anywhere a traditional gurney won't fit.

This innovative, yet simple product requires demonstration. The market wasn't big enough for television advertising, but the product still needed to be seen on a TV.

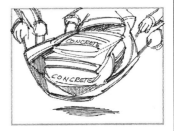

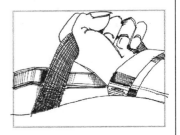

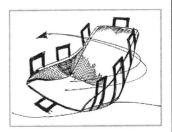

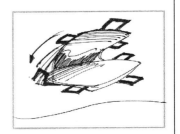

On-Air Lead Generation...Let People Sign Up To Be on Your List

When your market is big enough for broadcast, lead generation with DRTV is very effective. Our clients at System Pavers, who create custom paving stone driveways, and White's Electronics, famous for their metal detectors, both use TV in this role. In both these campaigns, TV "reaches out" to new people – people who would never be reached effectively with lists.

Why? In part because relaxing in their living rooms, viewer minds are more open to new ideas. And by letting the viewer call for a brochure or consultation, these companies put their consumers in control and their ensuing direct mail is more likely to be read.

All Your Television Should Be Online

Any TV you create should also be used online. But, there are some critical lessons about online video that the broad market has yet to learn. Importantly, despite "viral video" hype, online TV can't live by itself. If it's to be effective, you have to drive viewership through your website, mail, email, PR, and other campaigns.

Say Something Meaningful in Your Online Video

In a fit of collective attention disorder, we are often told that "online video must be short." I disagree. And I'm not alone. In a surprising result, a recent study showed that when viewing commercial clips online, *younger* audiences prefer longer clips – and that's exactly the young audiences we're told won't listen to long messages.

We find this to be true every time. For the recently released U•be™ salon hair weave product, we created a twelve minute in-store piece that lives online in a short segment and a long segment. Online the long "how to" section is viewed six times more often than the short piece. Why? I think it's because online viewers want answers and they know that a "how to" video is usually where valuable information can be found most often.

Despite digital advances, studies are showing that well executed direct mail campaigns readily outperform most of the new media. And that means there's no better time than right now to begin to make persuasive TV a core part of your direct mail campaigns. ▼

What DRTV Success Tells Us About Brand Advertising

Infomercials are the only TV advertising that consumers *choose* to watch. After all, when consumers see traditional TV spots, the choice they've made is to watch a program – not the spots.

If no one watched infomercials, it wouldn't matter. But, consumers stop to watch infomercials in massive numbers.

So how do infomercials achieve this level of success? And what lessons should brand advertisers take from those of us who have learned how to create infomercial success?

1. *Consumers respond to advertising that helps them make smart purchase decisions.*

   In research, consumers complain about the lack of information at retail stores. They laugh at the idea that traditional advertising helps them make purchasing decisions. And, while the web offers a wealth of information, it doesn't offer effective demonstrations of how a product impacts their lives. Infomercials succeed by offering consumers something they aren't getting anywhere else – communication and demonstration that make products meaningful.

2. *Effective communication is a process.*

   Traditional advertising usually limits itself to a single "big idea" or mere "lifestyle" messages. By contrast, infomercials persuade consumers through a communication process – moving them from initial awareness to purchase. A long form show does this by layering a set of core messages so that each uncovers a deeper understanding of the product. It's the layering of these messages that make infomercials so persuasive.

3. Product understanding generates far more value than brand.

Atomic's Drill Doctor infomercial spent years on-air and drove over two million unit sales. And the campaign built so much price support consumers willingly paid $100 for a product that sharpens 25-cent drill bits. By contrast, traditional brand advertising rarely generates dramatic price support. Why? Consumers pay more for meaningful products than for mere brand. (And even better, they pay the most for a meaningful product with a good brand.)

4. The creative idea cannot become more important than the communication.

DRTV only succeeds when consumers pick up the phone. And by counting phone calls, we've learned that humorous DRTV spots generally don't work. We've learned that DRTV messages must be carefully oriented around the product and not simply a lifestyle. And, we've learned that storymercials generally fail. Why? Clever ideas can satisfy the creative team without bringing meaningful communication to the consumer.

5. Consumers only need about 15 seconds of concept.

When agencies stretch 30-second spots into 30-minute shows, they fail. Why? Traditional advertising is based around big conceptual statements that are important, but quickly absorbed. And once interested by the concept, consumers want to know more. Unfortunately, traditional agencies rarely offer more. And when they do, it's usually only product features. Successful infomercials offer much more. We fill thirty minutes resolving objections that might stand between consumer interest and purchase and showing how a product becomes meaningful in a consumer's life.

6. Positive messages are most powerful.

Too often, traditional advertising starts and stays negative. But overall, infomercials are a generally positive art form – where products promise clear results. DRTV spots rarely spend more than 10% to 20% of a commercial defining the problem. Why? Because advertising delivers higher impact when it communicates positive messages.

7. Don't just "do" research – listen to it.

Infomercial agencies succeed much more often when they are skilled at listening to research and executing it. This means that focus groups can't be about verbatim transcriptions or tallying up "how many said what." And research should never ask consumers to critique creative choices or discuss "likeability." Research must focus on how messages change consumer perception of a product — something you learn by putting down your pen to watch and listen.

8. Ask people to take action.

Perhaps afraid of the answer, traditional advertising rarely asks consumers to take action. But infomercials always ask consumers to take significant action — often purchasing the product. And experience proves that with the right understanding of a product and the right offer, consumers will take that action.

9. Don't take a campaign off the air too soon.

Phones tell us when an infomercial stops working. By counting calls, we find that strong campaigns produce the same phone results for years. This suggests that traditional advertisers cycle advertising too quickly. Brand advertisers should resist the temptation to change strategies or campaigns just because they want something fresh.

Successful DRTV has moved beyond yell & sell. And that has expanded DRTV far beyond its early days.

Now traditional advertisers need to overcome their prejudices and listen to the lessons of DRTV. Then who knows, consumers might even begin to choose to watch traditional advertising. ▼

The Truth About Common DRTV Myths

Myth: *DRTV is seen only by midnight munchers and insomniacs.*

Truth: **Most DRTV advertising airs between 5 am and 11 pm.**

Myth: *No one I know watches DRTV.*

Truth: **Over 60% of consumers watch DRTV. Why? We give consumers the info they need!**

Myth: *TV buyers live in trailer parks.*

Truth: **Research shows DRTV viewers cross all demographic and lifestyle categories.**

Myth: *Success in DRTV requires direct sales.*

Truth: **DRTV is advertising. So it drives the biggest profit at retail. Some DRTV advertisers don't even try to sell on TV!**

Myth: *Brands don't use DRTV.*

Truth: **Rubbermaid, Sharper Image, Sears, Hamilton-Beach, AT&T... (need we say more?)**

Myth: *When you use DRTV, you join Ron Popeil and Tony Little's club.*

Truth: **You could if you wanted to! But I wouldn't work with you.**

Myth: *Your creative options are the following:*
Yell & sell, yell & Sell, Yell & Sell.

Truth: **Yell & Sell techniques are often the easy way to hock a product, but not a good choice if you want to create long-term sales and a trusted brand.**

Myth: *Only mass market products work on TV.*

Truth: **Hmmm. A successful eight-year TV campaign for the Drill Doctor – a $100 tool that sharpens 25-cent drill bits. Talk about niche success with DRTV!**

Myth: *DRTV success requires a 300-pound ex-pugilist or a former actress.*

Truth: **Don't worry about celebrities. Atomic makes your brand the celebrity.**

Myth: *Television viewership declined over the past few years.*

Truth. **The latest research shows that TV is as popular as ever. During primetime, you'll still find two-thirds of American households watching TV.**

Myth: *TV's effectiveness has been decreased by DVRs.*

Truth **According to the Journal of Advertising Research, with or without the DVR, normal viewer behavior is unchanged. Some people view all ad messages, some pay partial attention, and others completely ignore commercials. A DVR simply allows a viewer that normally would've ignored advertising to simply fast-forward past it.**

Myth: *I can just put my video work on YouTube and I'll sell lots of product.*

Truth: **It's easy to post on YouTube. So we wish you well with your 15 viewers. But if you want to have real impact with video online, you need to drive people to care to watch it.**

Myth: *We have no interest in direct sales so we can't use direct response style TV (DRTV).*

Truth: **Direct Response Television (DRTV) has emerged over the past decade as one of the most powerful communication tools for building retail sales. That's right. We said retail. Direct sales are no longer the most important reason to use DRTV, because it builds sales, higher margins, strength to negotiate with retailers, and strong long-term business. ▼**

Is DRTV Right for You?

Listen to some marketers and you'd think that DRTV lived in a separate universe and was effective only for crazy people who yell at their audience or light cars on fire.

The truth is, DRTV is just TV advertising – with a direct method for action. And that means DRTV should sit at the table with other options for brand advertising where it offers unique strengths.

At the same time, merely slapping an 800-number on a brand spot doesn't deliver the benefits of DRTV – thousands of examples show it can't. Instead, it is critical to learn of situations where DRTV's unique strengths come to bear in order to mix this medium with your other media options.

The following section explores ideas for the types of products where DRTV can play a significant role in your marketing mix. We start with the example of one high tech company – so hip and happening you'd think it had moved beyond any need for DRTV – with the article "Google Needs an Infomercial." And, yes, I'm quite serious about Google's continuing opportunity to grow using long form direct response television.

Google Needs an Infomercial

Driving Consumer Electronics Success With DRTV

Google needs an infomercial – a half hour paid program. So does Kindle. And so do many new technology products made for consumer use.

The value of most technology is hard to see and hard to understand. Infomercials reveal that value, showing consumers why the technology is meaningful. Even better, infomercials do this while reaching a mass consumer audience as well as the growing market of home based businesses.

Why Google?

Google is an excellent example of a company whose technology has outstripped their communication. Google engineers have put heart and soul into a dizzying array of online products that position Google for excellent additional profits. Except, the innovations are unknown outside Google and a few early adopters. As a result, this superb technology asset underperforms financially.

Google could capture this lost opportunity if they chose to communicate with an infomercial. And when they did, they would drive short-term profit while building brand value that would box out future competitors.

From Bold Risk Taking to Risk Avoidance

In my nearly thirty years in and around technology it's always been clear that the companies who take the smartest risks develop the most exciting new products. But once they start to communicate, tech companies often lose this boldness – leaving superb technologies to fail through risk aversion.

Creating DRTV

What should you do to take advantage of this untapped opportunity? Of course, avoid cheesy "yell & sell" techniques used for skin care or fitness.

Instead, evaluate an array of large and small agencies remembering a few key pointers:

- Be thoroughly strategic. An investment in strategy and research up front will dramatically increase your success.

- Don't be distracted by long lists of clients – lists that may reflect a long list of failures. Look, instead, for your agency to be a long-term partner.

- Only consider agencies that listen to you, don't invent creative strategy in the first meeting, and will be able to articulate something that your current team hasn't been able to articulate.

- Avoid agencies whose work looks and feels like extended versions of 30-second spots. While **you** might enjoy viewing your 30-second spot stretched to 30-minutes, consumers won't watch it long enough to hear what you have to say.

- Look for an agency that integrates your infomercial with your other PR, traditional media, social media, and online efforts.

Many technology companies seek communication safety with the local outlet of a multi-national agency. This agency's name may make investors happy. But for new products their work nearly always fails – because "award winning" advertising rarely moves consumers to action.

Other companies dislike the investment required for communication. So they try to succeed on the cheap, hoping that consumers will organically discover their products through online osmosis or social media. (I love the power of social media. But it's not a good way to drive the release of new products.)

Infomercials "Cross the Chasm"

To understand the power of an infomercial for technology, consider the "Chasm" model from Geoffrey Moore's book "Crossing the Chasm." Moore identifies the large chasm that separates the earliest "Innovator" buyers from the much larger "Majority" markets.

In my experience, the only companies that cross the chasm quickly have good in-depth communication. Hence infomercials – and they can work whether your product is software or hardware, Internet based or mobile services, B2B products or mass consumer products.

Did You Really Say "Infomercials"?

Some technologists think they've moved "beyond" something as old school as television – much less paid programming. But they haven't. Today's TV is more vital and alive than ever. And today's technology infomercials feature innovative, high quality products.

These infomercials are exciting, fresh, and highly compelling. They engage consumers with vital and up-to-date messages. And, by capturing the interest of a mass audience, they drive activity everywhere – online stores, brick and mortar retail, mobile service consumption, and catalogs.

An ROI Medium

Infomercials deliver outstanding ROI and are one of the lowest cost ways to reach a mass audience. When executed to sell directly, profits from sales can pay for most, if not all, of the media investment. When used to acquire new customers, infomercial lifetime value is generally higher than the value of customers acquired through other channels.

Even better, they introduce new products faster and with more strength than traditional advertising methods. And they build your brand by ensuring that consumers understand the outstanding value you offer. ▼

....

My agency developed a spot for Limbo 41414's mobile SMS reverse-bid auctions. This creative concept was based around an animated :60 spot which tested successfully and had excellent DRTV lead generation rates.

Limbo SMS Reverse Auctions

VO: How low can you go?

You might get an iPod for sixteen cents like Ben Milam did playing Limbo 41414!

Or win a flat screen TV for $3.25 like Jason Koller.

And Sondra Peterson just won a Hummer for $36.65!

Sondra P: Everybody can play this game, even someone like me

VO: Play Limbo today and you could be the next big winner when you bid on a Mini Cooper.

How low will you go? Text Mini to 41414 on your cell phone to start playing.

If your bid is the lowest and only bid at that price by the end of the auction… you win!

Text Mini to 41414 now!

It's fun to play Limbo….

Testimonial 1: My winning bid was $5.80

VO: It's easy to play Limbo…

Testimonial 2: My winning bid was $2.60!

VO: Start playing today. It's FREE to bid. With no spam or hidden charges – ever!

So grab your cell phone, because someone will win this Mini convertible on June 2nd.

Text Mini to 41414 and play Limbo now!

Storyboard	Finished Spot

Your Hit Brand DRTV Product May Already Be on the Shelf

Over the course of my career in DRTV, I've watched many brand marketers seek to leverage DRTV's retail power for their brand and fail miserably. While it's true that DRTV will invigorate retail sales, equally important is knowing how to identify the right product.

The Simple Truth

There is a surprising, simple, and powerful truth in DRTV – the next megahit is already on the store shelf.

The George Foreman Grill, the Popeil Showtime Rotisserie, the Drill Doctor, and even the acne treatment ProActiv are based on products that existed well before TV brought these products to life.

Each of these campaigns added smart packaging, merchandising and communication to existing solid products and turned sleeper products into compelling consumer megahits.

What Should Brands Do Differently?

Once we accept that the next product is already on the shelf, the DRTV equation changes dramatically – and becomes less risky. There are thousands of products on the shelf that lack only the vision, savvy, and investment needed to drive massive retail sales with DRTV communication.

To find those products, here are five key guidelines:

- Look for products that have lackluster sales but are **passionately loved** by consumers. This behavior indicates a disconnect between what consumers "think" a product will deliver and its value – a disconnect that DRTV communication can bridge.

- Look at products that only sell when consumers walk into the store looking for them. DRTV can be the engine that drives traffic seeking the products.

- If you think your product message is "old," **challenge your assumption**. Marketing teams often dismiss products because "that's been tried by our competitors" or "we've already done that."

- If a product was the belle of the Housewares show and the entire industry was talking about that idea in 1994, that "buzz" probably never made it to consumers. DRTV supplies the communication that makes the difference between success and failure.

- Look for products with important and complex benefits. When these benefits are successfully communicated, the result is high margins and long life at the retail store.

An example is the ProActiv acne treatment. ProActiv's active ingredient is common in acne products you find in about any store. But, Guthy-Renker had the vision to package it right and the savvy to build DRTV that drove that message to the market. The result? Another lackluster retail product reached massive market penetration on the shoulders of DRTV.

Remember That DRTV Leads to Surprising Success

Few brands can imagine the power of DRTV to radicalize their markets. Short form reaches out to consumers with basic communication that drives retail and supports it with TV sales to offset media costs.

Even better may be the long form opportunity. Long form offers the chance to radically change the market with high margin products that have long market lives. These products can lift a brand and company onto an entirely new economic plane.

Go for it. Look through the lackluster products sitting on retailer shelves. Then take a risk. Find the right brand DRTV agency, research the "winning" products, and take them to market. It's hard work and you'll find it challenging. But, be ready to ride the rocket that only DRTV can add to your brand. ▼

DRTV Makes TV Advertising Affordable for Niche Products

In the old world of the three networks, TV only made sense for mass market products. But in the world of 500 channels, this is no longer true. There is now excellent niche opportunity with television.

While traditional TV is too expensive for most niche products, DRTV delivers the same powerful communication at a dramatically lower cost.

In fact, DRTV is an excellent approach for niche products – *if* you sell through retail channels as well as TV, stay away from old-school DRTV and learn some key lessons from past niche success.

A Niche DRTV experience.

One great example of niche success is the half hour show for the Drill Doctor Drill Bit Sharpener.

This campaign was on-air for eight years and targeted a market so specialized that nearly half of purchasers owned arc welders. Despite this, Drill Doctor drove sales of over two million units. Critical to this campaign's success was reaching out to

....

The Drill Doctor infomercial first aired in November 2001 and ran for eight years. It is the longest continuously running tool infomercial in history. Fully one third of retail purchasers first learned about the Drill Doctor from the infomercial. Since the infomercial's release, over two million Drill Doctors have been sold between on-air sales and retail. And this is a $100 product that sharpens and 25-cent drill bit! ➤

VO: We buy expensive, big drills then blame the drill even though our problem's a dull bit.

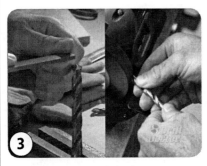

When things get really bad, we try to hand sharpen – with almost anything.

But the truth is, no matter how good your drill is…your drill is only as good as its bit is sharp.

HOST: You know, drill bits lose their edge a long time before they finally become dull and unusable.

But you'll probably find that most of the bits you use…

…they're not really sharp and not really dull either…

new TV purchasers. Fully one third of our TV sales came from people who had never bought from TV.

Niche product success requires new creative approaches.

Unlike the latest ab product, niche campaigns fail if they rely on common infomercial formulas.

But be careful how you break away from these formulas. Do *not* break away so that your DRTV feels more like traditional advertising. Rather, drop the formulas to make sure it communicates *with* your consumer and doesn't feel like "yell & sell."

We've found that new TV purchasers stay tuned to communication that's credible. But they turn DRTV off when they get a whiff of typical "BS" – like classic yell & sell or beautiful, overproduced testimonials.

Niche success requires unique media buying choices.

Relying on traditional media resources is the way to niche failure. So to succeed:

Don't use big media agencies. Big agencies usually can't put in the effort needed to make these smaller campaigns succeed.

Media buyer databases don't predict effective niche media. We find the stations suggested by mass market success often don't work well for niche products.

Cycle your media. With a niche product, a given airing may work, then stop working, then work again. So, plan to cycle your media and look for a media buyer who is willing to work in cycles.

Daytime. Around 90% of our airings for a niche product are daytime airings. Today's DRTV is no longer an overnight medium. DRTV has finally come into the light of day.

Before Walmart, there was an excellent network of specialty stores.

Niche products were regularly introduced and marketed through this network because it offered consumers a valuable experience not found at Walmart. The specialty network may have been overtaken by mass merchants, but DRTV can take its place and drive niche sales at mass outlets. ▼

DRTV Finds
What Nielsen Misses:
An Audience
That Will Take Action

Nielsen ratings are often attacked for a variety of problems with their statistical reliability and I certainly don't disagree with those challenges. But we should give Nielsen credit for reasonably estimating what is entirely unmeasurable: random acts of private TV viewing by more than 300 million Americans in more than 100 million homes on over 250 million TV sets.

Rather, it's Nielsen critics who need to take a hard look at things and see that *there's a more fundamental problem that goes far beyond statistics.* Namely that no rating system, Nielsen or otherwise, can find the most cost-effective media for reaching an audience that will take action – will go out and buy your product.

Enter DRTV – the surprising modern media engine that drives big change more cost effectively than any other TV. How? In part, by measuring how effectively each time slot on your TV schedule reaches an audience that will take action.

Let's Review Traditional TV Measurement

Traditional TV metrics start by giving us demographic descriptions of audiences (yawn) – and these descriptions dominate ratings. But the truth taught in advertising courses around the country (like my courses at Portland State University) is that demographics are the *least* effective way to locate a target consumer that will take action.

This is a problem that is well known, so traditional media planners have developed much more sophisticated ways to describe and target audiences. They've been helped along this route by research firms and the networks themselves who analyze viewer psychographics, lifestyles, behaviors, and geography. Traditional planners try to buy based on these criteria.

But notice what's missing: there's no way to know predisposition to take action.

By Contrast, Consider DRTV

In DRTV, we start with some planning using traditional audience criteria. Then, within two weeks of starting a campaign, we've looked at phone and web results and adjusted our media buy to target the media that drives the most cost-effective action. We repeat this process each week – honing the media buy to achieve 10%, 20%, even 50% to 60% improvements in effectiveness.

Then later we return and use traditional media models to evaluate our buy for the impact we've had and to get an even clearer picture of impact at the retail store.

For example, Atomic ran a cookware campaign where we found the most cost-effective results on Lifetime Movie Network. By contrast, several "traditional planning" networks performed quite poorly – Oxygen was 250% less, Food Network 400% less, and HGTV 800% less effective at reaching consumers who would take action. So after only two weeks, we removed those networks from the schedule.

The result? With a budget under $1M, in three months we drove the biggest cookware introduction at Linens-N-Things in their history. Let me say that again: we introduced a product nationally for a major retailer with under $1M in media spending and the result was the biggest cookware introduction in their history.

In fact, over a twenty year DRTV career, I've worked with many clients who turn to DRTV after getting minimal results from spending over $10M in traditional TV. And when they turn to DRTV, they usually drive ten to twenty times the unit sales at retail with less than half the spending.

Does Predisposition to Action Matter This Much?

Absolutely. Let's assume we randomly select one hundred people who fit your best and most in-depth target market description. How many of those are likely to be brought to action? A half? One? Two? Perhaps three? Experience shows that if three out of one hundred people from a target market are ready to take action, you've got astronomical market potential.

With traditional planning, you are choosing how you spend tens of millions in media without knowing whether the people you reach are the same ones that will move to action. If we choose American Idol because "that's what our target watches," that's also all we know. We know nothing about how cost effectively advertising on *American Idol* will reach people who are likely to take action.

A company with media money to burn can choose to ignore this reality. No one else should. Because in case after case, DRTV campaigns drive massive results at retail, more cost effectively than with traditional planning while also building brands and changing brand perceptions. ▼

Start with Research
for On-Air Success

As you consider products and strategies to drive your DRTV program, research should always be included. And look for two things from this research. First, learn about whether your campaign can be successful. And second, learn what it takes to be successful.

Not all DRTV agencies understand this. One of my employees attended a talk by the head of a large brand DRTV agency. This executive claimed that there is no reason to do research early in a project. Why? It hasn't helped increase success at his agency.

That's a stunning admission for a brand agency. Early research is thoroughly proven to increase results. My team uses it to deliver success in nine out of ten campaigns.

At the same time, I'm not surprised by his comments. Tapping the power of research in advance of a project requires a sophisticated sense of communication. Too many DRTV decisions are made by production teams that aren't trained in these advertising skills.

Trial and Error Is Not Research

There's a seductive argument given for skipping early research that goes something like:

> Consumer research is conducted in an artificial situation. So it can't be trusted. What we can trust is whether people buy the product. Therefore, the only reliable test is an on-air test.

Let's be brutally honest. On-air testing tells us nothing about why a campaign did or didn't work. Even worse, by the time you're on-air, you can't afford to fix the creative because you've already blown your production budget.

Early Research Has the Most Impact

Research money should be spent when and where it can make the most difference. Early in the project it can guide big issues: messages, creative approaches, production styles, and the offer. Early research also builds critical guidelines for thousands of quick decisions about scripts, testimonials, actors, staging, graphics, and directorial choices – decisions that make the difference between success and failure.

Avoid Common Research Mistakes

One reason many DRTV agencies avoid early research is that they don't know what to do with it. Some firms even conduct research to please their clients despite knowing their own teams will never make use of it.

Testimonial development teams may want to do your research but take care. These firms specialize in getting consumers to say what *you* want them to say. Research requires listening to what consumers think and feel – even hearing things you may not enjoy.

Some agencies take short-cuts like having account execs lead focus groups – often in the agency lunchroom. In this case, your agency is likely to hear exactly what they want to hear – not the challenging truths that are critical to success.

The most pervasive research errors I encounter are with dial groups. Producers love dissecting their finished work frame by frame with the detail found through dial groups. Sadly, this detail rarely matters. DRTV fails because of big issues: how the product is presented, the credibility of the presentation, the value it claims to deliver, and how meaningful this is to consumers.

Learn Your Way to Success

Early research can't guarantee success – nothing can. But dedicating a portion of every budget to learning from consumers increases your chances dramatically.

Brand clients often assume their existing studies will work for DRTV. But general brand research usually can't give us the insights we need for DRTV success.

The most useful early learning comes from qualitative work. Surveys offer concrete answers. But only methods like focus groups reveal the heart and soul of the consumer.

Research: Make It Right the First Time

Too many clients come to us with failed campaigns that were created by agencies that reject early research.

Most of these products *should have been* successful. But it's often too late because wrong assumptions have made the work unsalvageable and clients can't afford to pay for dramatic changes.

So for maximum success, start your campaigns with research. Then ensure that what you learn is applied throughout the campaign in order to reap the maximum from DRTV. ▼

Why Focus Groups Remain Critical for Advertising Planning

I am tired of people giving credit to silly statements about focus groups. Focus groups are a powerful research methodology – certainly for the development of advertising. Like any research methodology, they can be misused. But well-designed groups deliver outstanding insight.

The most common attack suggests that focus groups are a problem because "people in focus groups influence each other." Of course they do and that's the whole point of a "group." When we don't want people to influence each other, we bring them in individually for mall intercepts or one-on-one interviews.

Groups developed because both experience and fundamental cognitive psychology proves that by themselves people can reveal limited truths about themselves. But when people influence each other in focus groups, they reveal more deeply buried truths that often emerge more clearly and more quickly. It's not a perfect method, but used carefully it is extraordinary in what it can discover. Even better, this information can be relied on to guide decisions that risk millions.

Research Fads

Consider, by contrast, the ad biz's latest fad: ethnographic research. By definition, ethnographic research is purely observational. Many times, it involves installing cameras then reviewing hours of tape to see what happened. This can be a great help in product design and it's useful for analyzing minutiae in human physical behaviors. It is a significant problem that subjects know they are being taped, usually know where the cameras are, and typically change their behavior as a result.

But true ethnographic research is very expensive. A cheaper version asks consumers to submit tapes of themselves and their activity. Having done this a few times, this shows us more about what people think WE want than about what we need to know.

And so, many projects use pseudo-ethnographic research where researchers parachute into a home to film, observe, and interview. Some claim that ethnographic work discovers deeper stuff because consumers are "put off" by focus groups. Right. Imagine that one, two, or even three strangers (interviewer, account planner, client) descend on your home with a video camera. They "hang" with all the intimacy found when complete strangers drop in to talk about deep subjects while filming the conversation. And what do they discover? Much less than they usually claim.

Focus Groups, Used Wisely, Discover Critical Truths

On the other hand when one person says something in focus groups (anything – perhaps something not very enlightening), it may challenge another to dig a bit deeper. And that challenges a third person, and so on. Then after ten minutes of good open discussion, we've uncovered truths that would not have been found without a group of peers. Of course, this also takes a research team with the skills to identify the important lesson – who knows when to ignore the most powerful speaker in order to hear the most perceptive speaker. (Sadly, this is a rare skill in many agencies where the loudest often win the arguments.)

In the end, I have listened carefully to the stories about the "amazing things" found through new research approaches. We all need to keep open to changes in techniques. But these stories typically have nothing to do with methodology. Instead, they show the results when researchers and clients become open to learning unexpected truths.

And that's the real crime in research. All too often, research is conducted with political goals – to protect a job, to prove that the agency is right, or to sell the boss on ideas.

So the next time you are approached to do some radically new type of research, stop. And ask for more challenging answers and more insightful results from the research you are already doing. ▼

Making Focus Groups Productive

It's an amazing set of dynamics that drive negativity about focus groups. Some people get tremendous political or new business gain from saying bad things about groups. Others don't like the uncomfortable truths found with good research.

But that's not the whole reality. There are significant errors in how some companies and agencies use focus groups. Here are some key thoughts from twenty years of research...

Provide Stimuli, Then Let Them Discuss

People in focus groups are most productive when they are responding to things you show them or ideas you put before them – pictures, statements, video clips, physical items, etc. Without this material, group discussion can become little more than an unedited Twitter feed.

As long as they are mostly on topic, let the people talk! I've seen moderators handcuff themselves to stepping through moderator guides. This is entirely counterproductive. The moderator we use has tremendous liberty to follow discussion and always ensures that we learn what we need to. With this freedom, she gets us more learning and we are able to do more with what we learn.

Deal with Important Topics

Even in phone research I find that consumers have a BS meter for importance. People will dig deeper and reveal surprising value when they are dealing with the important issues. On the other hand, if you ask silly questions you get silly answers.

As a result, groups are a poor place to compare minor textual variations in marketing departments' product position statements. As a guiding light, use some wisdom from direct response advertising: never test whispers.

Use Them for the Right Purposes – Not to Avoid Responsibility

Research learning helps us make responsible decisions with confidence. Unfortunately, many companies and agencies use focus groups to avoid responsibility by asking consumers to design products or to create ads in focus groups. This may help with corporate politics. But don't do it. It's our job to make tough choices.

Never rely on verbatim transcriptions of the discussion. The value of any comment can only be determined by sensitive observers who witness/view the group dynamics. Transcripts let teams cherry-pick comments which good researchers would ignore – usually picked for reasons of corporate politics or to avoid tough choices. (We carefully transcribe selected segments when our reports are going to be read by readers when English isn't their primary language.)

Never use groups to determine if people "like" your advertising. The mere term "like" always takes discussion off track. Instead, groups should learn whether ads change perceptions and move people toward purchase.

Two Keys: Moderator and Respondents

Moderator. Learning as a result of group dynamics is the sole reason you're using focus groups. So having the right moderator to tap into those dynamics is critical. You need a moderator who knows how to engage a group, knows your product or service pretty well, understands the marketing implications of your medium, and can think on their feet. And you need a moderator who can help consumers reveal deeply buried or carefully guarded opinions.

Respondents. With a good moderator in place, getting the right respondents is critical. If you don't have the right people, you won't find reliable learning. This, is not as easy as it sounds. A great recruiter, the right specifications, a foolproof screener, and much more are all critical to getting the right respondents.

Respect the Participant

Above all, the key to focus groups is to respect the consumer. The people who attend your groups aren't perfect. And they never know everything you wish they knew (and that's important learning of its own). But if you have a good moderator and good recruiting, I find that they express what they know, think, and feel with the right intentions.

Sometimes, respondent comments can make agencies and clients angry. This anger shouldn't be directed at the participants. If you never find yourself frustrated by what you hear, you are not digging deep enough and are not open to the extraordinary truths groups can help you learn.

In fact, what you hear from groups should sometimes be humbling. After all, marketing is a very theoretical discipline. And at some point, theory has to face reality. There are few ways to learn where theory and reality come together than with focus groups. ▼

The Shelf Potato

L et me explore in detail a situation where DRTV is of critical value: The "Shelf Potato." The Shelf Potato is a well-loved product – loved by the manufacturer, loved by the retail buyer who brought it in, and loved by the consumers who buy it. Except, not enough consumers choose to buy it.

These aren't rare products – and every manufacturer and retailer has to deal with shelf potatoes. Sometimes, they are the result of problems in the product itself, the market, or the price you're asking relative to the value consumers put on what it delivers.

But most often, it's a problem of communication – and the right communication can bring shelf potatoes alive – especially communication with DRTV.

Eight Reasons Products Sit on the Retail Shelf

Grills nearly identical to George Foreman's lingered on store shelves for nearly 20 years. Then, the Foreman infomercial blew the doors off, driving over $100M in sales in two years. And we learned that while the grill delivered tremendous value to consumers, no one had known of those benefits or believed it would deliver them.

Not all shelf potatoes have potential like the Foreman Grill. Some sit on the shelf because they should. The Microsoft Kin was released with massive communication, failed to show unique value, then lingered on the shelf only to be cancelled, leaving a black spot on Microsoft's reputation.

Why Potatoes Sit on the Shelf

How can you tell whether you have a Foreman Grill, a Kin, or something in between? Start by identifying the problems that keep it on the shelf.

Here's a list of the most common types of problems I've seen.

1. *Consumers don't know why they should care about the product.* We all have busy lives. And successful manufacturers reach out to consumers to show the value of the product through advertising and PR. It's an extraordinarily rare product that walks out the door when you do no more than put it on the shelf.

2. *Consumers won't find out about the product in their daily grind.* We live by patterns. Patterns as we move through a store. Patterns in how we live at home. New products must worm their way into our minds despite the fact that patterns often present a barrier. And that means communication that

reaches out to consumers offline. Be wary of pure online plays. These patterns are notoriously resistant to efforts to reach out with web based initiatives.

3. *The product is stocked in the wrong part of the store.* Some shelf potatoes can be brought to life merely by moving them from one spot to another. A friend of mine had tremendous impact moving certain food products out of the spice and baking aisle and locating them with the fresh vegetable section. We've all seen cases like this. And yet it's easy for products to sit in the wrong place when we fall back on rigid category thinking that is confirmed by the common silos found among retail buyer's.

4. *The retail operation can't support the product.* In mass retail, marketing must plan that most sales associates are so overloaded with products that the most you can hope they know is that your product exists and where someone can find it on the shelf. So if you have a complex product, like many technology products, it's your job to find ways to deliver the communication needed outside of retail.

5. *Your packaging isn't helping – and might even be hurting.* Ah, packaging. Too often we ask too much of it. And ironically, too often we ignore the opportunity to use it for communication. While ad agencies often aren't the right teams to design packaging, perhaps you should bring them together with your internal or external designers so that all of your communication gains power through integration.

6 *Sitting on the shelf, the price appears high relative to the value consumers perceive.* You can respond in several ways. Obviously, you could choose to decrease price. But the best long term benefits come through other approaches. How can you increase awareness of the product's value – thereby increasing the price people will pay?

7. *The product started well and lost momentum.* There are many reasons for losing momentum – one being that communication was pulled before enough consumers hear what they needed to know. But also, the exact product you start with should stay on the shelf for as long as possible. Otherwise, consumers get confused. (In technology, especially, companies grow tired of their product versions long, long before they lose effectiveness with consumers.)

8. *Product Disaster.* And of course, there's the ultimate problem: The product simply doesn't offer enough consumer value. In this case, it's better to cut your losses.

But Don't Walk Away

None of the problems can be solved for free. Otherwise, the products wouldn't be sitting on the shelf. But unfortunately, this fear of costs can lead companies to abandon shelf potatoes.

In marketing discussions, companies often minimize the development costs and exceptionally high risks in a new product development. So their fear of costs for shelf potatoes isn't balanced by an accurate sense of the costs and risks of new product investment. Because redeeming a shelf potato can be much less expensive, lower risk, and carry a much higher potential profit reward.

And this makes it fun to wander the back store rooms of manufacturers talking with them about their potatoes. Because there is tremendous potential for high profit margins sitting on the shelves in the store – as well as in their back rooms. ▼

Avoid Shelf Potatoes
—Do it Right the First Time

First impressions count. And a shelf potato has failed in its first attempt to make a first impression. That means that corporate and retailer politics may be stacked against efforts to make them come alive.

So, the most important lesson is that your best road to success is avoiding having new products become shelf potatoes in the first place.

How Can Products Avoid Becoming Potatoes?

Assuming you've done all your other homework right, the single most critical issue is supporting your new products with the right communication. So know when you need communication to drive a product. Then either supply that communication or don't proceed with introduction.

Research (with honest introspection) can help detect communication risks ahead of time. Negotiate carefully with retailers to ensure the right placement. And, avoid putting a product at mass retail before you're ready. Quite often, retail merchandisers will love a product but not be the best judges of the challenges it will face on the shelf.

Unfortunately, this simple idea turns out to be much harder in the reality of company operations.

Just One Experience

I once dealt with a classic shelf potato – a product where people who owned it loved it. But, without communication the product sat on the shelf.

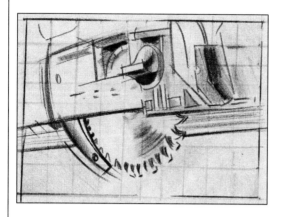

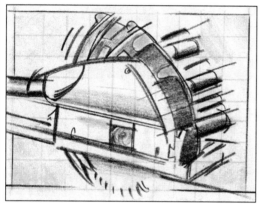

Sitting on the shelf, the Festool TS saw may look like an expensive circular saw. But it's more comparable to a $5,000 portable panel saw. We created a video to shift this perception. Then that video was used in direct mail, on the web, and in-store. Sales took off.

It didn't need to have turned out this way. We knew communication was critical from early research. And, in a key 8-hour strategic meeting, the entire team (marketing, finance, sales, development, production, advertising) concluded that this product should be introduced slowly – not with big box retailers until we had the right communication in place.

Except, one week later, the sales team sold the product into big box with an agreement to put it on their shelves day one. Despite this violation of management trust (another issue entirely), the company let the product hit the shelves without communication and without a strong plan for getting that communication out.

It took five more months after hitting the shelves to get communication in place. But by that time, the big box stores decided the product was a dud and kicked it out. Then, the product was cancelled because of big box's experience (and some uncontrolled costs from over-design).

What They Missed: Product Success

I know there are no guarantees in the world of new products, but this one would have sold with good communication. Instead, the sales team got greedy, placed the product on the shelves before there was communication to create demand, and that led to the failure. (It's a rare corporation that is willing to walk away from a big box order – even when it's against their best interest.)

So, care deeply about that first impression with your team and at your retail partners. But worry less about consumers, who are much more forgiving – and often never even hear about these products because they fail so quickly.

All too often, great products that have a poor first rollout descend into shelf potato status and never get the second chance that might bring them alive. ▼

The Politics of Potatoes

Assuming you have a product that has become a shelf potato and it looks like you can bring it alive, how do you get past the politics?

One general theme affects politics of potatoes: perspectives about money. When a new product is under development, companies seem to minimize the size of development cost required to hit the market. Yet the relatively minimal marketing costs required to redeem a shelf potato hit everyone's radar screen.

Your biggest challenge is shifting the corporate eye from the fresh, new thing to the reality of finding the highest returns for the lowest investment.

1. Know that anti-potato politics work against the corporation's best financial interest. That means you have a strong position – by staying focused on the money. If a spud can be redeemed, you monetize a past investment in product development. And that can be done for dramatically less money than creating a new product.

2. Watch the politics within marketing. Be ready and be patient. But don't back down from your fundamental truth: If you're right and the potato comes alive, it's a massive financial win for the company at lower risk than any new products.

3. Know that politics aren't just the one's in marketing. For example, finance teams are often paid to be conservative – to challenge assumptions. I don't resent this kind of pressure. Since you can discuss potatoes with firmer financial reasoning, you can win over the finance team if it's a solid proposition. And if its not a great proposition, then you've built credibility with the finance team by engaging in reasonable discussion.

4. Retailer politics are often most critical. Once a product has been on the shelf and failed to move, it's hard to regain trust. Your ability to make it past these politics is a matter of trust and your history with the retailer. It's also helped if the retailer has experience with similar challenges in the past. (BUT, this is also why it's so critical to succeed out the door.)

5. Politics are not generally a problem with consumers. Most shelf potato problems have stayed well off the consumer radar. Even in the case marketers would consider a massive high-profile failure (like Microsoft's Kin), mass consumer perception isn't likely to have turned against the product. Mass attitudes take years to build. So even though negatives generally build quicker than positives, consumers are the least of your worries.

6. "But Brand X tried this product, too, and theirs failed." I'm fascinated by this logic because it shows the way perspective gets warped inside an industry. Major releases from competitors dominate our view of the business – but not for consumers. A failure that appears large in our minds probably didn't even reserve a flea-sized spot in consumer minds. So while it's possible that failures are critical red flags I think it's likely that the product failed because of problems in execution – most often by failing to invest in the consumer communication required to make the product thrive.

If the politics in your operation are thick, you might wonder whether the potato has come out of the ground and into the french fryer.

But, don't let this stop you unless it's a fundamentally unredeemable situation. After all, your product's potential may be massive. George Foreman style grills sat on shelves for decades before launching into the retail stratosphere. Your company might have a similar gold mine already sitting on the shelf. ▼

Avoid Death by Brand Advertising for New Products

When you have a new product, the first order of business is getting consumers to love the product – love it so much they buy it.

Unfortunately, the ad/creative business is obsessed with brand advertising. And, sadly, choosing brand advertising for new products is a leading cause of shelf potato-dom.

Agencies tend toward "brand advertising" because they can focus mostly on making advertising that consumers "love." That makes for a fun creative process. Even better, brand advertising moves creative careers ahead quickly because they make such superb portfolio material.

But using brand advertising at the wrong time can kill a product introduction because brand advertising leaves behind very little communication about the product. Consumers buy products when they know why they are meaningful to them. If consumers aren't told meaningful reasons they'd want a product, then the product "doesn't exist" (no matter how brilliant your engineering team). And, if the product doesn't exist for consumers, then the profits don't exist either.

Five Key Steps Can Keep Your New Products from Suffering Death by Brand Advertising

1. *Make the Product the Hero.* It's all too easy for the creative process to focus on the wrong hero – the actors, the clever writing, the art direction, the movie-like experience, or the agency/creative team. Keep your products from becoming shelf potatoes by making the product the hero in the advertising.

2. ***Trust That Consumers Care.*** Traditional agency teams often believe that consumers don't want to know about products. I beg to differ. Love of product is a prehistoric human impulse – one that started when the first human kept a specific animal skin because it covered them better than other skins. If a product is worth inventing, people want to know what makes it meaningful.

3. ***Avoid the Staleness of Brochure Copy*** (but make great brochures). Product messages need fresh words. But, all too often the words around the product are as stale as those we find in most auto brochures (a waste of printing). Many creative teams and companies simply don't have the instincts to make product oriented long copy interesting. So they deliver dull and "expected" copy that consumers will never hear.

4. ***Make An Offer.*** The single most critical thing you can do for your brand is to get your product into consumer hands. So use directive language that says "buy this product." And make your communication so valuable to consumers that there's a reason to act upon it.

5. ***Use Agencies with a New Product Specialty.*** Most agencies don't have strong new product skills (though most will tell you they do). Most TV and video producers don't either. And most designers and art directors don't. With superb skills at crafting brilliant brand advertising, they don't know how to make the product the hero. So look for an agency whose work shows they make new products succeed or regularly take existing products to new markets.

Product-Oriented Advertising Breaks Through!

When you make effective product-based advertising, your work will break through the clutter – without women on bicycles trailing five feet of hair from their armpits (whose ad was that, anyway?)

Ads like these are typical of the disembodied creative that agencies create attempting to break through consumer consciousness with creativity alone – and without product connections. Except a stray but clever creative idea won't live in the consumer mind in a way that drives product sales (our minds don't work that way).

By contrast, if your development team is any good, then your product will be quite unique – highly differentiated so that it delivers meaningful advantages. And a creative team that relies on those advantages, finds creative that breaks through and sticks in the consumer mind.

And that means success – making your product a shelf potato candidate no longer. ▼

WebTV's Shelf Potato Story

Retail teams are asked by their management to generate the maximum revenue per hour. So new products struggle at retail because they typically require more sales time for the same revenue.

Consider WebTV. At this point, it's been around for more than a decade. And while it hasn't found a broad enough mass audience to dominate tech conversation, it has sold quite well to a niche consumer electronic audience.

But early on WebTV very nearly became a shelf potato. The Philips version hit the shelf in late 1996 supported by around $10 million in sexy :30 television spots. And, it sat on the shelf...and sat and sat. I have been told that it only sold when the regional specialists from Philips were in the store.

In the beginning, it took a specialist because consumers needed a massive information fix at retail. Unfortunately, in the same 45 minutes it took a salesman to make one WebTV sale, that salesman could sell three DVD players of equal value. So retailers didn't drive sales because selling WebTVs lost them money.

In this case Philips responded and in October 1997 they released a half hour infomercial for the product. And by mid-November, with only a few million in ad dollars, they had to take the infomercial off-air because they had sold out at retail. (And, of course, they put it back on-air as soon as the stores were re-stocked.)

Why did a few million dollars in infomercial time dramatically outperform over $10M in :30 spot time? The infomercial solved the communication problem that kept units on the shelf. With the infomercial on-air average sell time dropped from 45 minutes to 5 minutes and it no longer required the regional specialist.

What lesson do we learn from this? WebTV was a perfectly good product with a strong market potential. So lackluster sales don't necessarily say anything about the value of the product. And sometimes it's a matter of putting out the right communication for the product to fly off the shelves.

Cross the Chasm
to Avoid Shelf Potato-dom

Literature about crossing the chasm in technology is filled with reasons products should have been re-engineered, re-thought, or simply never attempted. But this literature rarely mentions communication. That's too bad. In my experience, communication – not product – may be the single biggest reason for chasm failure.

DirecTV's Chasm

I had the good fortune to do some strategic work early in DirecTV's lifecycle. Their initial marketing was all about technology. Digital picture quality and 250 channels dominated the discussion.

Our work focused on later consumers – not the earliest adopters. And what we found surprised DirecTV. Because we found that these later adopters didn't care in the least about the values DirecTV was using to sell their product.

This truth frustrated some of the marketing managers. (One demanded the opportunity to personally present the product in focus groups because she figured we just weren't presenting it right. We don't usually work that way, but it was good she presented. Because it made even clearer that the problem wasn't style but content.)

DirecTV was wise enough to learn from what we found. They realized they weren't showing enough product value for their next consumers to care to buy.

DirecTV's Solution

Their solution, the one that kept DirecTV from shelf potato-dom, was a combination of communication and packaging.

First, they leveraged their technology, but repackaged it into something sports enthusiasts around the nation couldn't get anywhere else: every football game from their favorite team.

Then, they rebuilt their communication to make this a primary value. (Of course, I'm leaving unspoken the fact that at the same time rural customers loved DirecTV because it was so much better than a satellite dish. But the rural market was never their primary goal.)

What Works for Early Adopters Usually Doesn't Work Across the Chasm

Take care as you consider this case to note that the early adopter values that DirecTV espoused were entirely wrong for the mass market they needed across the chasm. So their message had to change dramatically.

DirecTV very successfully used DRTV to help drive this communication change. In 1995, I helped DirecTV create its first full half hour infomercials. They continued to use infomercials in their mix for five more years. Then, as the product matured, they shifted more heavily to short form DRTV – a primary component to their marketing mix even today in 2011.

DRTV supplied an information channel for them that wasn't needed for early adopters who loved tinkering with new technology to figure it out. But their majority of consumers needed more – they needed to know why they should care and come to believe DirecTV could replace their cable.

In fact, if there's one clear lesson to learn about the chasm is that it's relatively easy to make technology that satisfies the early adopter. Later adopters demand a product value and clear communication that challenges marketing departments and baffles their traditional agencies.

So if you have a shelf potato, look closely to find the value that is meaningful to the mass market. Then tell them about that value as clearly and powerfully as you can – with the TV that is proven to resurrect the Shelf Potato, with Direct Response Television. ▼

How to Succeed with Direct Response Television

f you've made it this far, then you must believe that DRTV just might offer an answer to some of your advertising needs and be a good fit for your brand. That means, it's time to look at execution: How do you make sure you do it right?

In part, brand clients need to expect more from DRTV. Too often brands hire the first DRTV agency whose pitch merely "wasn't offensive" – perhaps surprised that we have some very smart people in this business.

The companies who leap too early pay for it with the bane of the brand DRTV business – campaigns where A-grade production covers up D-grade communication.

In this section you'll learn about Atomic's "Six Degrees" – a way to evaluate whether a DRTV campaign is getting maximum impact. You'll also learn a wide range of tricks of the trade for getting the results you want.

My hope is to lay a foundation for you to build DRTV campaigns that advance your brand, increase your profits, strengthen your relationships with your retailers, drive massive product sales, and in the end, move your brand forward. Because DRTV's true power should deliver all of these.

DRTV Drives Success
for Strategic Goals

It's Not Primarily About Direct Sales Anymore

Over the years, DRTV has been driven by a single-minded focus on TV sales. In this one-dimensional approach, the MER (ratio of TV sales to media cost) becomes the single most important measurement of campaign success.

In the hands of a master, this model has led to outstanding success. And so we are all saddened to note the passing of Billy Mays, one of the true masters of TV selling through short form. Unfortunately, when less skilled marketers focus on MER, they forget the brilliant insights that are the underpinnings of Billy's work. As a result they copy his style while missing his substance.

The One-Dimensional World

The copycat approach and one-dimensional pursuit of the MER has been used to justify a wide range of marketing sins. And the pressure to sell has moved many of these campaigns beyond exaggeration – leading to absurd claims, flat-out lies, directed testimonials, silly gags, and much more.

What our business rarely talks about is the horrendous failure rate of these imitations. Best estimates are that twenty nine out of thirty DRTV spots and infomercials fail to reach their MER targets.

Even worse, the mythology of the one-dimensional world has created a bankruptcy problem for long form DRTV. Many of the biggest TV sales successes have ended in bankruptcy or hushed and hurried company fire sales. This includes the Sharper Image, George Foreman Grill (Salton-Maxim), and Rotozip. I expect we'll have to add Little Giant Ladder and FEIN Tools (USA) to the list in a year or two – but that's just a guess.

Testing the MER Driven Myths

I've been fortunate to be involved in campaigns that have tested the MER theory. In one case, a client developed two shows for the same small kitchen appliance. One followed the MER myth and used slicer/dicer presentation along with traditional infomercial talent and methodology. The other was a more carefully crafted and more sophisticated infomercial. The net result? Both shows drove the same MER. But the sophisticated show had better total impact because it didn't alienate consumers.

And today my team is running a campaign that avoids the usual formulas but is selling just as much on TV as its TV competitors while driving four times the sales per media dollar at retail. Think about it: *four times* the impact for the same budget. Why? Because we avoid cheesy techniques and formulas that alienate retail purchasers.

Expanding DRTV's Dimensions

One surprising DRTV industry truth is that smart industry insiders with long term success have generally only gotten there by expanding beyond a single dimension. Guthy-Renker, for example, has become dominant force by reducing its dependence on high MERs – shifting to consumable products with long-term revenue streams (e.g., skin care). Unfortunately, many DRTV agencies and consultants advise clients poorly – not yet recognizing that success in DRTV requires multiple dimensions.

In fact, DRTV success requires acknowledging that the one-dimensional model doesn't work for everyone and that there are more subtle and more nuanced approaches – approaches that don't sacrifice TV sales while delivering higher long-term impact.

There are many ways to describe this type of campaign, but my own agency's pursuit has led us to develop an approach with **six major goals** rather than just one. We call our goals the "Six Degrees" and they clearly include TV Sales (or MER). But more importantly, they add measurements for effectiveness at driving retail, developing long-term brand value, and overall communication quality.

DRTV Mythology Must Change

DRTV is a funny business. Despite claims to know all the answers, the choices most DRTV producers make are driven by a set of myths – myths based on lore and not on fact. But it doesn't have to be that way.

When you add dimensions to DRTV, dramatic things happen. First, TV sales can be excellent (this alternative approach isn't about losing TV sales). At the same time, immediate sales grow across all channels when offensive gimmicks that drive consumers away are eliminated. And equally important, meaningful brand value is built that can be turned into bigger future profits.

For people who've been around DRTV for a long time, moving away from the one-dimensional myth into a multidimensional world may be hard. But newcomers who choose to embrace the full power of DRTV will find a much more powerful business than the industry's failure rate would suggest. ▼

What is "Brand"?

"Brand" is one of the most abused words in advertising. From David Arnold's **The Handbook of Brand Management:**

[For a consumer] a brand is a form of mental shorthand. The main benefit is that it removes the need to shop around and devote effort to a [more] serious analysis of the choices in a product category.

Brands are made from four key elements.

- The **Promise** that the consumer relies on to make their choices.

- The **Product** (or service) that delivers the promise.

- **Creative** elements, which play a number of roles.

- Any and all consumer **Interaction** with the brand, the product, the ideas, and the promise.

Atomic's "Six Degrees" Approach to Getting Maximum Impact from DRTV

Having participated in the unprecedented growth of branded DRTV, I've seen the industry come a long way over the years. At the same time, DRTV is not yet delivering the brand impact – strategically as well as tactically – that our customers want, need, and of which the medium is capable.

The Six Degrees of Brand DRTV

So at Atomic, we've defined Six Degrees of Brand DRTV that have become a shorthand way to help us evaluate the effectiveness of our campaigns.

1. *Longer Time Formats.* DRTV is perhaps best known for offering longer increments of time in which to demonstrate to consumers the value that a product delivers. This ability to spend time talking about the ways that products affect consumers' lives offers a unique opportunity to communicate important strategic messages that communicate a brand's promise. Unfortunately, aesthetic judgments easily lead DRTV campaigns astray so they become simply longer (and dull) versions of traditional advertisements. So the first measure is how well a campaign makes use of the longer time formats.

2. *Communicating To Heart and Mind.* Having more time brings increased opportunity to build the brand's inherent value via emotional connections. This lengthier communication gives time to connect emotion, brand, and product to increase impact. Unlike traditional advertising which, given the time constraints, has to choose between emphasizing emotional connections or the product – DRTV allows time to do both well. When you connect product, brand, and emotion within the same advertising you create deeper messages that build a more mature brand relationship with the audience. So

our second metric judges how effectively our advertising touches both the heart and the mind of the consumer.

3. *Immediate Direct Response.* All brands "promise" things to consumers. But, promises only translate into solid brand value when they are fulfilled – when the consumer interacts with or purchases the product or service. The third opportunity DRTV offers brands is that it prompts consumers to take immediate action – calls come into the ubiquitous 800-number or, nowadays, web hits. Tactically, that immediate response generates direct sales that offset or subsidize the cost of the advertising (making DRTV one of the few forms of advertising that even an accountant can love). However, immediate response is even more important strategically, because consumers have bonded more strongly with a brand when they have moved beyond simply listening to messages to taking action. So our third metric measures the level of direct response we've generated.

4. *Measurable Response At Retail.* DRTV's prompting of the consumer to take immediate direct action via phone and/or web simultaneously creates strong and immediate impact through all sales channels, particularly retail. We measure the speed of this response across the channels (in-store, Internet, catalog, etc.) with controlled testing, linear regression analysis, and consumer surveys. So, for example, we typically see between five and twenty units sold at retail for every unit sold directly by telephone. Once again, this tactic translates into strategic power, because one consumer taking positive action is more significant than hundreds or thousands of advertising "impressions."

5. *Inexpensive Media.* DRTV is purchased on a special rate card so it is the most cost-effective television advertising. We find that campaigns deliver results at half to one quarter of the cost of other media. (A second reason DRTV helps you build good will with your finance department!) Even better, profit from direct sales can help offset media costs (or even pay for the entire campaign). Some brand DRTV campaigns deliver up to ten or twenty times more impact, net, per media dollar. So, this tactical advantage of DRTV takes on strategic importance because it is worth millions of immediate dollars for additional media purchases.

6. *Brand Execution.* Our final metric evaluates whether a campaign has achieved great brand communication at two levels. The first level is brand basics. Will viewers recall the brand and connect it to the product? Are fundamental brand elements executed thoroughly (e.g. logos, colors, styles, etc.)? Does your consumer know the name of your brand?

The second level considers whether the campaign leverages the unique, and more sophisticated, brand communication that DRTV can deliver. Does it enhance the believability that this brand will deliver on its promise? Does it expand consumer understanding of the promise? Does it fit the product, and therefore brand, into the viewer's life in new ways? Does it make the promise more memorable? Does it connect the consumer more emotionally with the promise? Do people know exactly what they're going to get?

Many campaigns execute the first level well, but few execute the second level. Only when a campaign executes fully on both levels does it deserve a high rating in this category.

Fully executed, these six degrees create strong brand messages that move beyond merely changing consumer knowledge or attitude to something much more important: changing their behavior.

The State of Brand DRTV Today

To evaluate today's DRTV against the six degrees, we've taken some typical campaigns and ranked their performance in each of the six degrees on a scale of 1 to 10 (where 10 means well-executed) then mapped the results onto charts. These charts make the challenge facing brand DRTV clients obvious.

Let's start with short form. Today, corporations are using short form DRTV much more often than long form DRTV. Figure 1 shows the weakness in recent short form campaigns from companies like Proctor & Gamble, Home Depot, Hamilton-Beach, and Black & Decker. These companies use excellent production techniques and use DRTV effectively as inexpensive media that drives retail. But their fundamental communication has been poor and doesn't take full advantage of the medium. We give

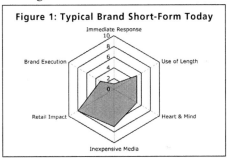

Figure 1: Typical Brand Short-Form Today

typical brand short form campaigns today a B to C- in communication despite their A in production.

Some brands have discovered the power of long form DRTV. Unfortunately, the campaigns created for these clients again use strong production values but lack

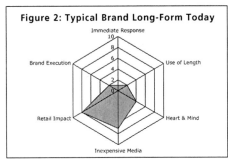

Figure 2: Typical Brand Long-Form Today

communication power. Examples of this weak communication can be found in recent work done for Bissell, Evinrude, Sunbeam, and, most sadly, the US Postal Service. The overall effectiveness of these Brand DRTV campaigns is shown in Figure 2. They are often little more than 30-second spots stretched for four or five minutes followed by more 30-second spots stretched for four or five minutes. I've reviewed this type of work for over fifteen years with many test audiences. Consumers find it dull and uninformative. When consumers are asked to spend more than five minutes with a brand, they want meaningful messages. (Otherwise, reality show re-runs are much more interesting.) These campaigns generally warrant between a B- and a D in communication despite their A+ in production.

The Future of DRTV

The future of DRTV lies in its power to build brand. And DRTV can only move from protecting brands to building brands when we fully optimize campaigns in each of these six key areas (Figure 3). When a campaign reaches this level, the result is highly-leveraged brand development that makes bigger changes in consumer behavior more quickly than traditional advertising, especially when introducing new products, repositioning brands, or expanding brands to new markets.

Today we have moved far beyond the old DRTV image of schlock and noise. In the process, though, the bulk of brand DRTV has become only "not bad." As a result, DRTV has not yet taken its place as an equal player among the options for building brands. But that, too, will come – when practitioners consistently create campaigns that move beyond the misleading idea that good production is enough and communicate brand messages with the power that only DRTV can deliver. ▼

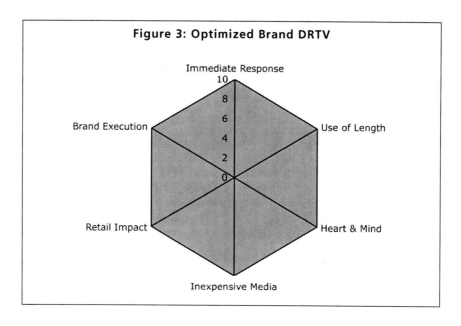

Figure 3: Optimized Brand DRTV

The Netpliance iOpener
– The iPad's Precursor

FEMALE HOST: The iOpener makes the internet as simple as a lot of things I take for granted. Like my dishwasher, answering machine, or my telephone. It makes the internet fun, practical and it's very affordable.

FEMALE HOST: For all the wonders of the internet, getting online can be challenging. And once you are online it can be frustrating to find what you need.

That's all about to disappear. Introducing…the iOpener. Now you don't need a computer to go online. This is all you need.

HOST 1: We were told to find a way to make the internet more useful at home. So we started with people. We went around the country and we asked them what they wanted. And they told us "make it easier to get online and make it easier to be online." So we set out to keep the iOpener simple.

The iOpener goes to the internet and checks for new mail throughout the day. Then, whenever it finds new mail, it brings it back to you.

When the iPad came out I knew it would succeed because of my experience with the iOpener in 1999. Netpliance's iOpener was a compact device dedicated to making email and the internet simple to use. This product took the Internet off the computer in the office and put it where it was most useful – usually in the kitchen.

Sharper Image Bankruptcy Is Warning Call to DRTV: Build Brands Now

Even If It Means Giving Up Some Short-Term Sales

In 2007 Sharper Image declared bankruptcy and sold their assets. This followed almost immediately on the heels of 7 years where they spent somewhere over $100 million on DRTV media.

So while I was saddened to read about the Sharper Image bankruptcy, I was also angered. The DRTV business must take notice of this failure. Sharper Image is just one example where a traditional DRTV megahit ultimately led to business failure – because they built no long-term future.

Salton-Maxim and the George Foreman Grill

After hundreds of millions of dollars in Foreman Grill sales, in a 2007 merger/sale, the Salton company was combined with Applica. And the company stock that had soared over $60 during the Foreman heyday, ended up priced under $2.

It is oversimplifying to ignore other business realities that may have contributed to this failure. But, their DRTV spending was an amazing strategic advantage – yet their infomercial delivered little long-term value.

Salton invested nearly $100M in media over the run of the Foreman infomercial. In return, Salton received no brand awareness and no long-term value. The primary beneficiary? George Foreman. To this day, consumers believe the Foreman Grill was invented by George.

Sharper Image and the Ionic Breeze

Starting in 1998, Sharper Image created multiproduct half hours that sold products from their catalog. The Ionic Breeze air purifier was introduced in a three-product infomercial. This show worked well and built brand value for the Sharper catalog while selling great products.

Then, DRTV industry experts advised them to shift to a single product format featuring the Ionic Breeze. Why? To get the highest short-term sales – the only thing the traditional DRTV industry really values.

So Sharper Image invested massive media budgets selling Ionic Breeze. And that left the company without a needed increase in brand value to support store and catalog sales. Compounding this error, messaging for the Ionic Breeze didn't support core Sharper Image brand values. (Although consumers knew they could get the Breeze at Sharper Image stores, I don't think they ever felt it made sense within the Sharper Image brand.)

Again, other business realities certainly made Sharper Image's life difficult. At the same time, their massive media spending produced little long-term value. It could have, and should have, been different. If Sharper Image had embraced their position as a catalog brand their shows could have built brand value by returning to their original plan.

RotoZip Tools

This story starts like the first two. A classic yell & sell infomercial drove exceptional short-term sales leading to excellent retail distribution. But, RotoZip was unable to leverage this into long-term success. A few years ago, they were quietly sold to Bosch. Word on the street is that they had to sell to avoid closing the doors.

What they should have done: RotoZip faced a more difficult situation than either of these first two since they had only one product. There were three key choices they should have made.

- Execute their advertising to create a RotoZip "brand."
- Reduce media spending to extend the life of the RotoZip product line.
- Bring out a second product line that would be easier to sell because it benefited from the established RotoZip brand value.

Lessons

The sad truth is that all these companies made a smart choice in selecting DRTV. We can only imagine what long-term brand power $100M in media *should have* brought Sharper Image, Salton, or RotoZip.

If you're approaching DRTV for the first time, let me make two recommendations:

1. Insist on your campaign building brand while you sell product. You can do both and you should. To maintain high long-term media budgets, you need sales from TV to underwrite media spending. And, you must have the discipline to make difficult choices to build long-term brand value – sometimes at the expense of short-term sales.

2. Be careful choosing vendors. There are a wide variety of "agencies" in DRTV with long lists of brand clients. Unfortunately, most are production companies or media buyers who take on the trappings of an agency. And, many of them can do no more for your brands than "do no harm." That's not good enough. Clients need agencies who build brand value.

Don't expect old-school DRTV players to change. But if clients and manufacturers pay attention and demand DRTV that is executed with brand savvy and sophistication, then they'll not only avoid the mistakes of Sharper Image, but build themselves a highly profitable future. ▼

Why Traditional Agencies Fail with Long Form TV

New media options and the hype surrounding online video has brought long form TV back into consideration for many ad agencies.

I applaud the productive thinking that recognizes how powerful long form can be. But, there's a problem – a big problem: *Most agency long form advertising isn't effective.*

Truth is that long form only works when consumers choose to seek it out and there's no reason to seek out most agency long form. Is there really any reason that consumers should seek out your long form?

Consider on-demand advertising offerings at TiVo or Comcast. Chevrolet and Porsche have used these venues to deliver highly produced sequences of cool car shots mixed with good music... and nothing new to a consumer. Yawn. They look like 30-second spots stretched to 5 minutes. Consumers won't seek out stuff like this.

What consumers want from long form is something they can't get in 30s – useful and complex ideas developed in ways that make brands more meaningful in their lives or help build stronger affinity for a brand by connecting ideas that can't be connected in shorter format.

Successful long form styles can range from product specific work to brand oriented long form. How much do consumers want this long form? My agency's half hour infomercial for the Drill Doctor generated a large enough TV audience to get a 1.0 rating in Nielson local marketing tracking – that's a 1.0 rating with a TV program advertising a drill bit sharpener! At the other extreme, my good friends at BuderEngel out of San Francisco have created excellent brand oriented long form TV for Levi Strauss, adidas, and Dr. Martens – airing some of that work on major cable networks.

Three guidelines lead to successful long form TV advertising:

1. *Long form must be so meaningful and compelling that viewers will seek it out.* Unfortunately, most agencies think "entertainment" is the draw that will bring consumers to long form. I think they're wrong and that "entertainment" is often the worst choice. When will ad agencies come to the realization that consumers want to learn about products and how they fit their lives? Sometimes an entertainment approach is right, but know that it only succeeds when it is extraordinary entertainment (à la the BuderEngel work).

This is a tough road to success. Networks spend years developing a sitcom that draws viewers. An agency won't succeed by simply hiring a "hot" production company to execute a treatment written by a junior creative team. There is no faster way to fail.

2. *Overcome traditional advertising practices.* Advertising experience often rejects messages that take more than 15 seconds to communicate. So, too often agency long form is a 15-second ad followed by "features." After all, what else would you put in long form? Well, not a list of features. Great long form makes a coherent, compelling message that evolves over ten minutes of great programming. If you do this, your clients will achieve results they could never have imagined from traditional television.

3. *Don't use the production companies you use for million-dollar spots.* Many production companies make 5-minute pieces. Few make them meaningful. So most long form produced for agencies lacks the meaning that consumers seek.

How important is all this? At the start of my career, I helped evaluate scientific computer systems for a major aerospace company (yup, I was a techie). We were besieged over a period of four years by vendors of all types and flavors. After the first year I had developed a firm rule about vendor meetings: *if the sales team arrives with a video, skip the meeting.* These "cool," high-production-value videos were a waste of my time. (Modern life provides thousands of opportunities to see "cool" production but few opportunities to learn new things about products.) Agencies mustn't train consumers to skip long form TV in the same way.

So ask this question of agency long form: Does it deliver enough meaning for a consumer to spend 4, 6, 10, 20, 30, or 60 minutes of their busy lives with it? Most agency long form doesn't. But if long form TV is to thrive, agencies must learn how to make the answer "yes." ▼

Long Form Distribution Options

TiVo: Two to five minute advertisements.

VOD Advertising: Up to fifteen minutes. Variety of national and local options.

Broadband TV: We may not be too far from P&G TV – all soap, all the time.

Streaming Networks: YouTube and more at many lengths.

Brand Programming: Meaningful programs are given good airtime. What can you create?

Paid Programming: Thirty minutes. Don't forget the lowly infomercial – the most productive version of long form today.

Your Website: Consumers who seek you out want to learn more. Offer it to them in long form video segments.

How Brands Can Make
Half Hours Succeed

There is a harsh reality in the advertising business: brands that attempt to use half hour infomercials regularly fail to change the game with this unique communication.

To be clear, brand half hours don't fail because infomercials are wrong for them. They fail because of mistakes in their execution – even top brands like Revlon, Sony, Corningware, and AT&T.

So while putting together guidelines for brand half hour success, I sought out researcher/strategist Carla Roberts. Carla is a former BBDO executive who has listened to thousands of research participants over fifteen years talk about half hour shows and what makes them compelling.

"It takes more than luck to create a successful infomercial," she observed. "It takes a new viewpoint, new research, solid goals, and a special agency with the right experience in the field."

Adopt a New Viewpoint

"Brand marketers think they know how half hours work simply because they've done other advertising," Carla continued. "Then they fail because half hour success requires a radical change in mindset."

Most advertising uses "Big Ideas" to create awareness over time. But an infomercial weaves together a number of ideas, concepts, and relevant facts into compelling programming that drives immediate consumer action. While not an easy feat, bringing all these elements together into a cohesive whole is the single most important ingredient in half hour success.

Understanding the unique opportunity and challenges from this longer communication is particularly vital because infomercial success or failure is clear right away – the numbers say it all.

Think Research

This mindset shift begins at the foundation – the research. Carla notes that brand research isn't enough to make a successful infomercial. "Most brand research looks at details in isolation. The research needed to create a successful brand infomercial looks at how details relate. So, it covers a massive landscape quickly."

This is the distinctiveness of half hour communication – adding up a range of concepts, details, and realities to build consumer conviction that the product delivers exceptional value.

Use the Full Half Hour

A half hour won't succeed if it's simply a 30-second spot with a bit more information and a patina of good filmography. True, a great half hour needs one or two compelling central ideas. But more important, it needs convincing details that connect those ideas to illuminate the product in new ways.

Where failed brand half hours are often light on content, "successful shows have coherent, substantive pitches which utilize every second of the 30-minutes," observes Carla.

As an example, in 1996, our team created a half hour show selling the latest Electrolux vacuum cleaner with extensive help from Carla. "They asked us to generate sales appointments for their door-to-door sales force," Carla recalls, "who would demonstrate a $900 vacuum in a marketplace loaded with $300 vacuums. We had to be so convincing that consumers would call to invite a stranger into their home to dump dirt on their rug then sell them something expensive to clean it up."

Research showed us where $900 in perceived value lay. Carla remembers, "we had to change consumer perception and build the idea of 'total cleaning power' then show how Electrolux's motor, fan, hose, and attachment design delivered it. Finally, we built even more value by demonstrating details of the product's exceptional design and usability." Consumers were convinced. This excellent branded half hour comfortably outsold the crass "yell & sell" shows of the time.

Solid Goals

Learning to communicate in the half hour format isn't enough. Many failures begin with goals that are unclear or aren't managed throughout the campaign.

Brands shouldn't shy away from selling on TV. A core group of consumers will buy from a half hour. And those that don't buy will retain the idea of action so strongly that there's an immediate increase in retail activity.

At the same time goals need to be realistic. Most brand campaigns are not profitable on TV sales alone, but drive ten to fifteen sales at retail for every sale on TV.

Finally, agencies need to be held to these goals. The focus on financial results is often lost when creative teams enter the campaign. Their strength is art – not numbers. Without a focus on results, failure becomes much more likely.

The Right Team

There's another key to brand infomercial success: the right team. This is extremely critical because an infomercial campaign is complex, integrating strategy, creative, media, telemarketing, and fulfillment as well as merchandising, product sourcing, and financial analysis.

And while big DRTV agencies have a wide range of resources, they're not always the right resources. Carla notes that "success doesn't come from having lots of people, but from a motivated, cohesive team who brings all the pieces together. I know only a few agencies that deliver this consistently."

A caution about the big DRTV agency myth of "media clout." Rather than a one-time upfront buy, DRTV media buys should be tweaked regularly based on daily reviews of results. So small, motivated teams of DRTV specialists often deliver better results than large agencies with "clout."

The Reel

Clients are often misled by reels because they only tell part of the story.

Carla notes, "It's hard to assess the value of a show from small clips. It takes seeing complete shows from an agency to understand whether they are compelling half hours and if the agency is good fit for the category. And, ask lots of questions to learn whether the shows generated solid results."

The Agency Question

Oddly enough, there aren't many "true agencies" in the half hour infomercial business. This is because early half hour suppliers were either production companies or media buyers. As the business has changed, many producers or buyers took on the title of "agency". But just adding the title and wearing black isn't enough – they still can't bring together the components to create and execute a successful campaign.

A final word from Carla, "I've seen the best successes from agencies small enough to hand-hold when needed and big enough to offer a full range of services. This means agencies committed to retaining clients over the long term – ones that don't take all the clients they can, but take good care of the clients they have." ▼

Wearever Builds Brand Success with Infomercials

Fall brings the introduction of new housewares in department stores – when a few weeks tell whether years of hard work succeed or fail. But The Mirro Company wasn't worried when it began its national rollout of the new Wearever "Allegro" cookware in July 2000. They knew Allegro would be a star.

According to Dave Merten then VP of merchandising at Mirro, this is the result of a strategic plan that included a 1/2 hour infomercial. Merten says the 18 months they spent selling Allegro on TV built retail demand – and retail margin. "Consumers know Allegro's value when they walk into the store. As a result, we're selling Allegro at retail for $300 – that's over $100 more than our traditional cookware pricing."

"Allegro challenges consumers with a unique shape that is squared at the top," continues Merten. "The infomercial gave us a way to help consumers understand the dramatic advantages for pouring and storage that result from this shape." Allegro adds flat lids that reduce messy boilover and double as strainers. And, it features a new non-stick surface that is "safe for use with metal utensils."

The Allegro infomercial rolled out in early 1999 and has sold well on TV. Media buys generally run 70%/ 30% (cable/broadcast). Says Merten, "Allegro fixes problems we found while watching tapes of consumers working in their kitchens. Our infomercial sells because it shows those problems then demonstrates how Allegro solves each of them. It's powerful communication."

Now, Merten looks to the future. "The long-term power for us will be using infomercials to develop our brand and support our margins. They will be part of our advertising mix for years to come."

After a promising retail start, the Allegro product was cancelled in a Newell/ Rubbermaid shake up which resulted in the loss of the entire Wearever brand.

Nine Lessons for Building DRTV Brands

Successful branding is alive, vital, and engaging. It is focused on how consumers live and how our products are meaningful in their lives.

But too often talk about DRTV branding becomes dead language – the language of established, bureaucratic brands like Budweiser, Nike, or McDonalds.

In DRTV, nearly everything we touch is new – whether products or brands. In our world, the arcane language of brand textbooks often hurts more than it helps.

So, I offer the following lessons for building DRTV brands. These lessons lead to stronger, more profitable brands. And, they start at the beginning: the consumer.

1. ***Consumers benefit from brands.*** Consumers make hundreds of decisions each week. Trusting a brand helps them make those decisions more quickly and more confidently.

   So market the brand like a product. Many DRTV companies build USPs (unique selling propositions) for products. What is the USP for your brand? Once you know, challenge your USP. Does it really make a difference?

2. ***Consumers must trust your brand.*** Consumers accept a brand when they trust it to deliver a specific product experience. But trust is a tricky thing. It has to be built.

   How? By making a promise, then delivering – every time. In a sales campaign, the product must exceed expectations. In a lead generation program, build trust with clear, useful information.

3. *Know your promise and stick with it.* Ginsu promised a great set of knives for $25. George Foreman promises quick and easy meat with less fat. ProActiv promises acne treatment that works.

   Then, never lose your promise through brand extension. Smart fitness companies rarely even mix aerobics and strength training in the same brand.

4. *Plan how you'll profit from your brand.* When a consumer trusts your brand, they'll buy future product with less marketing effort. Or, they'll pay higher prices. Or you'll get better retail buy-in. Or all three.

5. *Expand your vision of a brand.* Many of my biz-school students arrive thinking a name is a brand. But a brand name is merely a label. The true brand is the sum of each consumer's experience with the product, company, and category.

   This suggests, for example, that we should use telemarketing for better branding. Consumers won't trust the brand if they have a bad experience during their three minutes with your telemarketer.

6. *Be patient and use small steps.* Plan for three to five years of brand effort before you see dramatic profitability from branding.

   During this time, don't waste money on expensive "branding" spots. Add brand consistency to your everyday advertising so consumers learn your promise and product together. Then over-deliver – day-in and day-out. When you least expect it, you'll discover that you've built a brand powerhouse.

7. *Develop a consistent creative strategy for your brand.* Consumers need years of consistency in order to learn about a brand. What consistent elements build the brand? A look? A feel? A sound?

   Don't trust DRTV producers to manage creative strategy. Guthy-Renker usually does smart brand work. But the producer for the Pilates show has projected four different Daisy Fuentes personalities. And their new order slate looks like Popeil's Pocket Fisherman.

8. *Develop your brand with consumer research.* Marketers often decide what we want, then try to force the consumer to accept those ideas. This "inside out" approach to branding will only succeed by accident. To plan for success, learn what your consumers need and deliver it.

9. *Celebrities may be bad choices for branding.* The first question from many DRTV marketers is "who's the celebrity?" A celebrity might make it easier to start a brand. They can also quickly overshadow the product.

   It can be more effective to use actors with great personalities that reflect the brand promise.

Branding is treated with nearly religious reverence in most advertising agencies – a reverence that too often wastes money on irrelevant advertising.

By contrast, DRTV creates highly informed consumers through tens of millions of dollars spent on 30-minute shows – informed consumers that quickly become brand advocates.

Claude Hopkins wrote *Scientific Advertising* in 1924. In his chapter on naming, he lists seventeen successful brands. Eighty years later, eleven remain top consumer brands, including Vaseline and Kodak. Will your brand be on the list in 2084? ▼

Case Study: The Kreg Jig

Problem
Kreg makes joining wood simple. Even more importantly, being able to join wood is the gateway to an entire realm of building. However, the do-it-yourself market was not aware of Kreg, the simplicity of building with Kreg Joints, and how the result opens up an entire world of building and repair.

What We Did
Atomic first developed an in-store sales video. Then we used the video for sales-oriented research. This research clearly showed that the Kreg was a strong solution for DIYs who wanted to build with wood but had been intimidated by the expertise they feared they needed to be a "woodworker."

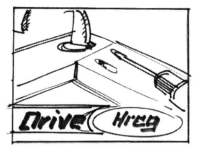

Our half hour show demonstrates how easy it is to build quality wood projects with Kreg regardless of the skill level of the builder. (After all, as the show states, "if you have a drill, a saw, and a Kreg, you can build about anything.") And, this show expands Kreg's brand by building the promise that Kreg is a company with woodworking knowledge DIY's can depend on.

Results
During the dramatic start of the economic crisis in the fall of 2008, Atomic's new ½ hour show for the Kreg Jig was tested and beat the on-air sales goal by 20%. The show has dramatically increased web traffic and retail sales and the Kreg Jig quickly became, and still is, a top tool at Lowe's, Rockler, and Amazon.com.

Measuring DRTV Audiences

DRTV is a "return on investment" advertising medium and today we learn amazing detail about a small portion of our audience – the ones who pick up the phone and call.

But *phone calls alone measure less than one percent of DRTV's impact.* If ten consumers purchase a product advertised on DRTV, only one will use the phone. The other nine will purchase at retail, by catalog, or on the Internet. Then, for every ten who purchase, another 1,000 are persuaded by our message.

What DRTV needs is complete ROI measurement. But before laying out the steps needed to obtain those measurements, we need to recall why complete ROI is so important. And why the Nielsen system will never serve the DRTV industry the way they serve traditional advertising.

Why Is This Critical—Now?

If Ron Popeil didn't need audience measurement to sell the Pocket Fisherman in the 70s, why do we need it now?

The industry has changed. Media rates are up significantly. Many retail product introductions are timed to coincide with an infomercial's release. And, in our research, we find that consumers view infomercials and DRTV spots today knowing they can skip the 800-number and purchase at WalMart, Target, or Home Depot.

The days of astronomical direct sales are gone. Campaigns no longer generate 4:1 to 7:1 media ratios. Now, more than ever, campaigns must be evaluated for their complete ROI – not just TV sales.

What *Shouldn't* We Do?

The wrong approach for DRTV would be to develop a system like the Nielsen system used in general advertising. True, Nielsen measures TV audience size. And, Nielsen numbers are discussed in corporate boardrooms around the country as if they were absolute. But Nielsen has serious weaknesses for DRTV.

Nielsen ratings were created for the world of three major networks. But DRTV thrives in the world of 500 channels. On 497 of those channels, programs don't draw enough viewers to get Nielsen rated. So Nielsens are generally ineffective when you're buying national cable. Or when you're buying the smaller of six or more local stations. And because of the economics, Nielsen is unlikely to improve their ratings quickly.

We should also be cautious about rating systems because they typically lead to media price inflation. Traditional advertisers pay a premium in order to know the audience size. That premium doesn't make sense in DRTV.

You Can't Compare Infomercial Ratings with Spot Ratings

Ratings are also a problem for DRTV because their meaning changes as we shift advertising lengths.

The half hour Drill Doctor infomercial regularly pulls a "1" rating or higher in local markets. In Portland, Oregon, a 1 rating means 1% of our 1.1 million TV households (or 11,000 people) watched the Drill Doctor infomercial for at least four minutes out of a consecutive ten-minute period. (Attracting 11,000 individuals to watch four minutes of an infomercial about sharpening drill bits. Amazing!)

Spot or short form media is much different. A spot is not rated – the show within which the spot runs is rated. So viewers don't choose to watch your spot – they choose to watch the show. And, since individuals only have to watch four minutes of any ten-minute period of the show, some program viewers were surfing for Baywatch reruns when your spot ran.

Estimating the Complete DRTV ROI

What we need most in DRTV is a solid estimate of complete advertising ROI – including some audience size estimates. There are four sources for this ROI estimate. Savvy DRTV advertisers should use all four.

Response Measurements

Response by phone is critical. Without audience measurements, response is the only way to be certain that we're investing our media millions wisely. And, experience shows that if DRTV doesn't generate a minimal response, then our advertising probably isn't too effective at retail.

Having said this, the DRTV industry needs to become more sophisticated about the range of responses it considers effective. In modern DRTV, many highly effective campaigns run with media ratios below a 1:1 (media ratio = TV sales divided by media cost). How low should we accept? Experience suggests, that below a 0.4:1 ratio, it becomes difficult to make good media choices.

Audience Measurement (Limited)

If your media buyer is purchasing effective DRTV time, very few of your media dollars will have a large enough audience to generate Nielsen ratings. (You will find more ratings for spots than half hour infomercial campaigns.)

You should use any ratings you can track in order to estimate the CPM for your campaign. You may be surprised how much less expensive DRTV advertising can be than print or radio.

But, do not rely on network supplied "audience by time slot" reports or the upcoming DVR (TiVO) based ratings. Both are skewed and highly inaccurate.

Tracking Research

Most major manufacturers mount periodic surveys among product purchasers in order to track influence factors. This research should measure unaided and aided recall of advertising influences.

In one of our campaigns, these measurements showed that one third of all buyers first learned about the product through the DRTV (unaided recall) and that just under 50% of all purchasers had seen the DRTV (aided recall).

Other, and more in-depth, research should also be used. In the above campaign, later research surprisingly showed that one third of consumers who purchased by phone had never purchased from TV before! (Another expansion that's needed for DRTV industry growth.)

Retail Impact

Unlike traditional advertising, DRTV's orientation to action generates an immediate response at retail. This makes it possible to use linear regression to analyze local market testing and estimate the impact at retail.

More campaigns should be doing this form of testing and analysis. But regression analysis provides a conservative estimate so it won't detect all of DRTV's impact. In our experience, it is only reliable for the first weeks after media airs even though DRTV consumers are still buying at retail twelve months after they see your commercial.

The Impact of a Complete ROI

Developing complete and standardized estimates of ROI will grow the DRTV business.

Traditional advertisers are holding media dollars back from DRTV until they can obtain a complete ROI. And many product categories are rejected by DRTV business because they don't generate an immediate profit from telephone sales – even though a complete ROI would show that they thrive in DRTV.

DRTV is a powerful medium which has only begun to realize its potential. And we need reliable estimates of total ROI to realize that potential. Once these estimates are in place we will find amazing new sources of growth – to which there are almost no bounds. ▼

Thoughts on New and Social Media

This book is not intended to cover all the topics surrounding ways to integrate DRTV with your other media. But here in 2011, we are in a time of tremendous hype about social media and other new media. Media change and rumors of change dominate discussions about advertising. So it is difficult to write about DRTV without commenting on these emerging trends.

I embrace new media wholeheartedly – both personally and professionally. And, my campaign classes at Portland State University regularly leverage new media as part of their finished work.

I hope this gives me both perspective and the beginnings of a clear-eyed understanding of both the potential of new media and the tremendous exaggeration that drives it.

As the dust is settling, TV continues to be the big dog of advertising – the only medium that can drive massive change quickly and at low cost. In fact, new media discussion would be helped considerably if the digital advocates had any significant television experience, because they'd realize that many of the successes they celebrate so freely are merely tiny advances in the broad fabric of advertising.

The following articles come from my blog and reflect my own attempt to embrace new media while balancing the hype with a healthy dose of common sense.

"Most Consumers Don't Want to Be Your Friend" and Other Axioms of Social Media

We've been sold the grand myth of social media marketing based on some rather flakey ideas. In particular, the ad biz has somehow convinced itself that the vast majority of consumers have a driving desire to be a company's friend. A new study* suggests there are significant limits to a company's potential intimacy with its consumers.

This study started by looking at consumer relationships with qualified counter help – like the people at an airline counter. In studying physical behavior and shopping behavior they concluded that people very often avoid idle counter help and opt for automated systems (like ticket kiosks or supermarket self-checkout). Building from this work, they researched other consumer relationships with companies – including social media. In the end, they conclude that the *majority of consumers really don't want to be close to most companies.*

This study is not unusual. In his recent book *How Brands Grow*, Byron Sharp of the Ehrenberg-Bass Institute lays out an exceptionally persuasive case for the low-involvement level that most consumers have with brands.

This Is Just Common Sense

Consider any consumer. They have a lot of brands in the house. But remove the commodity brands and there are probably a few hundred brands where a signifi-

---

* Tom Ryan. "Self-Service Trumps 'Live' Service".
  http://www.retailwire.com/Discussions/Sngl_Discussion.cfm/14870,
  November 18, 2010

cant connection is even a consideration. And, there's little reason to want to be friends with *any* of them.

What is the value to the consumer from connecting with Dial Soap? Or Cascade Detergent? Or Sony? Or Levi's, Ethan Allen, Sherwin Williams, Dania, Ikea, Nintendo, Lego, or... It simply isn't worth the social media and email clutter.

Even when passionately connected with a brand, many consumers don't even want to be their friend. Why? A company is not human. And our connections with brands are fundamentally economic in nature – not social.

Axioms for Social Media

This leads to a set of key axioms about people interacting socially with companies. The current research points clearly to these axioms. But research into social media has been conducted primarily with wide-eyed awe and avoided the tough questions. So these are labeled axioms because they are based on intuitive jumps and aren't "provable" based on hard numbers.

- Most consumers don't want to be your friend. They may like you. They may even love you. But that doesn't mean they want to be connected with you online.

- Consumers who will be your friend on Facebook or any social media outlet are a very small segment of your target market.

- Consumers who will be your "friend" are usually not those customers who generate the most money for you.

- The influence of active social media consumers is overstated. There is no reason to believe that consumers who will be your "friend" are important influencers – nor your best influencers. (This conclusion comes from some excellent research[*] on the "Million Follower Myth" that I've written about elsewhere.)

- The vast majority of consumers have at most a handful of companies or brands where they will build social connections.

- The most powerful social media connections are through narrow social media – like your company's social media site. It's always been true in marketing that focus delivers higher returns. Somehow, we need to rebuild that understanding in social media.

What Does All This Mean?

Social media is exciting. And it's here to stay. As companies evolve their marketing, it's very smart to plan a social media strategy. But social media agencies are

---

[*] Meeyoung Cha, Hamed Haddadi, Fabricio Benevenuto, Krishna P. Gummadi, "Measuring User Influence on Twitter: The Million Follower Fallacy", www.twitter.mpi-sws.org, May 2010

using classic "FUD" salesmanship – casting fear, uncertainty, and doubt on your future "unless" you spend a lot of money with them.

In fact, there is a big danger of social media work taking both energy and budget away from more highly profitable investment opportunities. This danger is made higher by the consuming nature of social media work. I find that staff who work on social media become quickly hypnotized by their new toy and lose their sense of perspective.

But most fundamentally, what this means is that with social media, as with all advertising, the most critical step is developing a clear strategic plan that leverages an integrated media strategy for the most business profit – whether today or in the long term. ▼

Five Reasons Consumers Will "Friend" Your Company

While we're looking at the people who will be your company's friend, what motivates them to become your friend?

In fact, I see five key reasons people will friend your company. And this starts by looking at the value they get from connecting with your company.

Coupon Clippers. Many consumers friend companies to seek discounts and deals. In other words, they are the coupon clippers. Interesting. Coupon clippers are powerful short-term revenue opportunities. But historically they have less brand loyalty and are of lower lifetime value to companies.

Party Animals. Many consumers friend companies because of clever "entertainment" (typically unrelated to product value). This is especially true for brands who make entertainment the focus of their online experience. Truth is that a significant portion of Party Animals are unlikely to ever use or purchase the product. One great example of Party Animal social work was Old Spice's 2010 campaign. Their online campaign generated massive social media interaction and ad business hype. But, analysis by *Advertising Age* indicates that, despite hype to the contrary, it had no detectable impact on sales.[*]

Groupies. There are some consumers who become professional fans or groupies. And, this happens for every company – not just the "hip" ones. The volume of groupies can be increased with effort. And, they are a lot like rock star groupies – emotionally significant to the company, but they won't fill an arena and they won't make your numbers for the year.

---

[*] Found in… http://dsgarnett.wordpress.com/wp-admin/post.php?post=1081

Customer Care. Many consumers connect with companies to seek customer service. One article I read this year pointed out that this is akin to "protecting your investment." If you own a Toyota and are concerned about this year's safety problems, you are more likely to friend them just to be up to date on recall notices.

Brand Engagers. Some connectors are truly engaged with your brand and will use social media to maintain contact. My axiom is that for broad-based social media (e.g., Facebook) this last group is important, but unlikely to be more than 10% or 15% of your total social media connectors.

What Does This Mean for Your Advertising?

I can't tell you what portion of your social media "friends" will fall into each category. That will depend on many factors including the design of your efforts to attract friends and the fundamentals of your product, brand, and category.

But when you look at that group that gathers around your company, some generalizations are quite reasonable.

- The hype surrounding social media far outweighs its economic value to companies. I think it is quite common to find that no more than 5% of your target will even entertain a social media connection. The further fragmentation into five categories makes each segment quite small.

- As a result, it's quite easy to spend your money chasing around after your least valuable consumers.

- If you want your social media relationships to be significant to your company, then you need to avoid the hype and the easy answers in creating social media connections. Instead, take some lessons from the direct marketing world and embrace the social media efforts that build solid and long-term relationships.

In no way do I think you should stay away from social media. But whatever your efforts, enter social media with your eyes open. ▼

U•be™ Hair Weave Cap

SHOOTING BOARD ROUGH.

① A.AMER. FEMALE HOST O.C.

MEDIUM   C/U   W/CLIENT

② YVETTE DEMONSTRATIONS: ON THREE WOMEN

CAP & HAIR APPLICATION

CAP   HAIR   HAIR C/U

STYLING DEMOS:

COMB   BLOW   CUT

ROTATE & REVEAL:

MODEL 1   MODEL 2   MODEL 3

COULD THIS USE A BEFORE & AFTER, MAKE-OVER TREATMENT?

FEEL THE HAIR:

FEEL   STROKE   TEASE

③ INTERVIEWS: STYLISTS

YVETTE   A.AMER.   CAUC.

④ 2-D GRAPHICS:

⑤ 3-D GRAPHICS:

GLUE   AIR/VENT.   PATTERN

CTA   GRAPHICS   TRIBAL/CIRCLES

⑥ STOCK PHOTOS:

PERHAPS A MIX OF EVERYDAY PEOPLE, AND CELEBRITY LOOK ALIKES:
BEYONCE, M.J. BUGH, IMAN, ETC.

....

The main ingredient for producing and shooting any type of video is visual planning.
It helps your team stay on the same page and keeps the project focused on strategy.

Offline Advertising Drives Online Growth

If you are pure B2B or consumer marketer with extremely limited goals, then you may be able to live online without encountering its tremendous limitations. But if you need to drive growth in large markets, then you need to look carefully at what's happening around you.

Consider Angie's List, eHarmony, and GoToMeeting. All are perceived to be pure "online plays." Yet each surprisingly uses massive TV advertising campaigns to drive growth. Dig a little deeper and we find that Zappos gets the highest online sales per customer when consumers receive printed catalogs.

And our list goes on. TV plays include GoDaddy, Vonage, and Hulu. I even saw a report recently that nonprofits with extensive online interaction commonly see the highest donations from offline efforts like direct mail.

Fight Back Against the Online Cult

Many in the ad biz have drunk the Kool-Aid of the cult of online advertising. At some point they bought into the idea that "all online" was the future. (In part, agencies buy into this because while it may not make their clients much money, it has tremendous impact on *their* bottom line.)

And now, rather than finally recognizing online limitations, social media fantasies have become the latest excuse for never leaving the web. (This, despite strong and conclusive research showing that consumers DON'T get new product learning from social media.)

Offline Media Is Powerful

Most often, I've found that online purists haven't experienced the power of traditional media... power that moves markets... power that drives mass results fast... power that can be exceptionally cost efficient... power that far exceeds what's possible in the cloistered world of online, social media, mobile, email, and other media hyped "cool" options.

And it's this power that so many online companies now rely on from offline media – because it drives growth.

What Limits Online Advertising?

Online advertising's limitation is that people have to know they want your product before it's effective – they have to know what you make and why they might want it. Online resources are superb for searching out answers to questions and sometimes purchasing the product. But online's generally a poor medium for driving out a message about something innovative and unusual.

This is critical if growth is your goal. Growth almost always requires getting your message out to new people, in fresh ways, in order to bring them to become interested in your product.

It's fundamental: if you are an online player and want to grow, you need offline media.

Consider Apple

Apple is not always a perfect marketing example. But they clearly understand the limitations in online advertising. In fact, online companies have complained for years that Apple doesn't spend enough of their advertising budget online.

That's interesting. Let's look at their growth here in 2011. In fact, Apple seems a lot smarter than those who suggest they need to do more online advertising. By observation, I think Apple figured out that PR delivers all the online presence they need and their advertising dollars are more effectively dedicated to TV and other mediums.

In truth, the companies who thrive without offline advertising are few and far between. And growth for your online (or offline) business may require that you move into your future by first looking offline. ▼

Online Fragmentation: Web Advertising's Incredible Blind Spot

In the late 1990's, the tech industry hype machine went into overdrive telling us that the web would replace retail and become the biggest sales channel for every product on earth.

Of course, it didn't happen. Today, brick-and-mortar retail dominates purchases – and does so while using the web as one of many communication options and as a small, but important, sales channel.

What's the hype machine telling us about advertising?

The same hype machine has re-emerged and is leaping at social media, viral campaigns, and online video as the magic that will rescue the web from a minority role in advertising. (This would, of course, bring all those juicy advertising dollars to the companies and their VC's who are behind the hype machine.)

Once again, these broad claims are bunk. And, with beautiful irony, the theory of web dominance in advertising breaks down because of what the hype machine also tells us is the web's biggest strength: nearly infinite segmentation.

Web users sign on, search through a small number of search engines, then scatter around the web faster than particles pushed outward from a supernova.

Web advocates have rightly noted that this makes the web ideal for targeting – claiming that online promotions can have laser-like accuracy. (This accuracy requiring, of course, various forms of passive and invasive tracking of your every online action.)

Segmentation and fragmentation are two sides of the same coin.

If all we expect of the web is a highly targeted minority role in our marketing mix, then the web has segmentation. Or if you are selling a niche B2B product to a technical audience (like IT), then the web offers segmentation – and highly valuable segmentation.

But segmentation becomes fragmentation when we consider the idea of replacing advertising's biggest gun: television. When compared with TV, web audiences are not merely fragmented but shattered into billions and billions of tiny shards. TV's opportunity to move millions of consumers to action simply doesn't exist on the web.

Consider it this way. If on its best days TV creates a power of 100, on its best days the web creates a power of 1 to 5. As a minority share of an integrated marketing plan, this "1" is important. But no matter how hard you try, the web's 1 can never replace TV's 100. (Or print's 75, or direct mail's 30, or radio's 60, or outdoor's 40, or...)

This becomes clear when you look at the big picture.

Sadly, if web advertising is all you've ever known, crawling around to gather enough shards to create micro-segments from nano-segments might make you think you are doing something big. (After all, it's a lot of work and mere busyness can easily mask ineffectiveness.)

But if you have traveled the much wider world of traditional advertising, you'll realize it's impossible to use online shards in mass advertising to create anything more than a very nice minority role. (Apple is just one example of a savvy advertiser who knows this and relies heavily on TV while using Internet advertising in a limited role.)

But heck, many web investors don't want to hear this. And, just so, they'll fire back. With what? Probably an industry research report showing an astronomical 20-year growth curve for the NEXT web invention – perhaps location based search engine optimization delivered via socially viral online video with a Twitter core hosted on a cloud. Yup. That's the ticket.

It's time for the ad biz to grow up and confront the tech machine's hype with advertising reality. ▼

Afterword

I hope this book has offered a unique understanding of DRTV and its potential. And perhaps you've caught some of the passion that I have for what it can deliver. So after all these pages, what more would I want to add? Let me offer three brief thoughts.

Mass Marketing is More Important Than Ever

In the face of considerable effort to convince us otherwise, mass marketing remains the key to brand success. In his book *How Brands Grow*, Byron Sharp[*] rejects anecdote and looks, instead, for brand truths based on hard statistical data. Using this data, he finds a great many things that challenge fundamental marketing assumptions.

Most importantly, he finds that brands grow big NOT because of the sales to their most dedicated consumers. Instead, brands grow big by selling to a very large number of new consumers. The implications of this reality are staggering and they clearly show that mass marketing remains where it has always been – at the core of brand success and driving significant change.

Even more importantly, this increases the critical importance of DRTV to brands. Because DRTV is the single most cost effective means for mass marketing.

A Focused Message is More Important Than Ever

New media has fragmented communication. Now consumers are confronted with a barrage of commercial message pieces – making it their responsibility to pull those pieces together into something meaningful.

---

* Byron Sharp, *How Brands Grow: What Marketers Don't Know*, (Victoria: Oxford University Press, 2010)

DRTV offers a solution. Longer communication times combined with the ability to leverage TV at low cost makes it a refreshing antidote to the "blipverts" that surround us. And a focused message dramatically increases impact.

Branded Salesmanship Is the Key to DRTV Success

If you choose DRTV, you will not be alone. You can learn from other brands that have seen the opportunity within DRTV and pursued it.

If DRTV failed them, it wasn't usually the result of outright failure and it didn't lack good-looking creative. Most often DRTV delivered results that were merely okay.

Merely okay is not good enough. Brands should demand that DRTV deliver MORE than they could get from traditional TV. Otherwise, why move into this unusual and demanding medium?

You see, DRTV is not like other advertising. You can't hire creatives straight out of portfolio school and throw them on a job. You can't even hire experienced traditional creative teams and truly tap DRTV's power. You can't accept D-grade communication just because it's delivered in an A-grade production. And you certainly can't succeed with a team who, no matter how long their client list, lacks a subtle understanding of salesmanship.

Instead, you need to build a vision of a positive and vital salesmanship that supports and builds your brand. That is true salesmanship – the ability to weave powerfully persuasive messages that lead consumers to buy your products while leaving behind a creative and vital brand message.

Embrace DRTV

So embrace DRTV for all it can deliver. Demand that your agencies dig deeper for true inspiration. Demand that they move beyond failed formulas and seek the unique communication that brings your sales alive. Demand that your agencies use the smartest DRTV media buying rather than handcuff them with corporate mandates.

And then, sit back and enjoy the ride. Because DRTV can do for you, your product, your company, and your brand what no other advertising can do: change the game. ▼

Acknowledgements

Special thanks to the clients who, committed to growing their business, have given us opportunity to show the impact these ideas can bring. Thanks to my team at Atomic where I've had opportunity to explore and clarify these ideas. Especially, John Gurney, Skye Weadick, Shelby Brill, Jack Rubinger, Don Lewis, Carla Roberts, Tim Hill, and the rest of our creative, production, media, and campaign teams who bring so much of their own passion to our projects. Thanks, also, to Dan Zifkin, Roger Delaney and the team at Zephyr Media who deliver more wise investment for the media dollar than any team I know.

Thanks to all the passionate experts I've been fortunate to work with who, as leaders in their fields, have helped me learn to recognize my own vision and its power. Thanks to Tom Haire, John Yarrington and the rest of the Response Magazine team who support the need for the DRTV business to evolve into its future potential and have given me an opportunity to have my voice heard. And last, but not least, thanks to my family, especially my wife Judith, who helps me along the way and whose support has been so fundamentally important to my success in this demanding work.

About the Author

Doug Garnett serves as Chief Executive Officer of Atomic Direct, an industry-leading full-service direct response television agency involved in all areas of Creative, Production, Media, Research, Strategy, and Campaign Management.

A respected expert in advertising communication and television, Garnett is a sought-after spokesperson for industry trade and business media where has written for numerous publications and has spoken at trade panels and symposiums.

Garnett brings a unique variety of experience to the challenges of DRTV. He started his career at General Dynamics where he worked on the Atlas and Atlas/Centaur rockets as well as the Space Shuttle. After leaving GD, Garnett shifted to marketing and sales where he sold Unix-based supercomputers, then typesetting software – a move that launched his career in marketing and advertising.

Doug lives in Portland, Oregon with his family and is an adjunct professor of general advertising at Portland State University. He writes regularly on his blog and for *Response Magazine* to share his vision of how brand marketers can leverage the power of TV.